In memory

of

Major Thomas John Goodman
M.B.E. R.E.

1914 -1974

	Chapter	Page
	Foreword	4
1	Amongst The Ranks 1929 to 1939	7
2	B.E.F. Dunkirk	20
3	Bomb Disposal Years	37
4	Special Operations Executive	57
5	Services Reconnaissance Department	74
6	Operation Ethelred (British Pacific Fleet)	95
7	Post War Bomb Disposal	103
8	Special Forces Club	112
9	PYTHON, India & Singapore I	115
10	Egypt & Suez	125
11	Singapore II	140
12	Western Command No 1 E.S.D. Plant Troop	150
13	The Retirement Years	162
14	UXB Film Synopsis	170
15	Acknowledgements	173
16	Reference List – Books, Videos, etc.	174

Forward

This account was begun during the COVID lockdown of 2020 after the garden had been manicured, the under eaves cupboards emptied of countless boxes, redundant "stuff" around the house had been ditched and the garage shelves rationalised.

For almost 50 years, my Father's document bag that I inherited after his death in 1974 had lain unexplored in various locations. I had thought about going through it properly on a number of occasions over the years to see what it might reveal, but somehow I had not been brave enough to face the emotion associated with it. Also, until Lock Down, there had never seemed enough time to sit down and examine its contents in depth. In 2020 that opportunity arrived, in spades.

When I rummaged in my study cupboard one day, in the early summer of 2020 to see what else could be disposed of, my Father's document bag fell out onto the carpeted floor. The spilt contents included a small number of documents from his Army days and a few family papers, including birth and death certificates. There were also several photographs of my father standing together with a mixed military and civilian group in front of what looked like a large country house. The photos were obviously taken during World War 2. There was also an "S.O.E. Record of Service Form", containing just his personal and next of kin details that had been completed in his own distinct handwriting and dated 1st November 1943.

My attention was grabbed.

What follows is the result of my journey into his past, triggered by that document case spillage. Inevitably, the scope of my research widened as various family threads came to light. My aim has been to record, and share, what I have found in the hope that it does not become lost to the generations that follow. I have asked myself, many times during the course of this endeavour, why didn't I spend more time talking to my family members when they were alive? I now realise it would have been a very interesting and enlightening experience. No doubt I won't be the first, or the last, to reflect on that sentiment. However, in my Father's case, it must be remembered that the Official Secrets Act drew a veil over the activity of organisations like S.O.E. for 50 years. It wasn't until 1995 that this veil was lifted, by which time my Father had been dead for 21 years. In any case, like very many of his contemporaries, he was told to "keep it a secret". Being an Officer and a Gentleman he did just that. So, even my asking may not have revealed the exploits I have discovered.

Researching my Father's exploits has included acquiring over 120 books and other material, including films and his personal records from the M.O.D. Several of the books include direct references to him, by name and his Army number - see Chapter 16.

The considerable power of the internet has also come into its own in this quest. The Australian National Archive, The National Archives at Kew, various S.O.E and Military interest groups, and their websites, have also yielded information through personal visits and the internet. However, not everything that may be found on 'the Web' should be taken as entirely correct. Cross referencing has proven absolutely necessary to validate the facts and to flush out any inaccuracies. I have found that is all too easy to be misled by well intentioned "red herrings".

Any infringement of copyright incurred in producing this is account is completely unintended, which itself has not been compiled for commercial gain.

At the conclusion of my writing this account, it is exactly 50 years since my Father died on 21st October 1974.

Ubique is Latin for "everywhere" and is the moto of The Royal Engineers.

Jerry Goodman

20th October 2024

(1st revision)

Chapter 1 - Amongst the Ranks - 1929 to 1939

Thomas John Goodman (Tom) was born in the Military Families Hospital, Devonport, Plymouth on 4th December 1914. He was the first of 8 children. (Fig 0)

As the eldest of the Goodman children, Tom was responsible for *"looking after his siblings on the street"*. He was taught how to box by his father, Thomas (senior), who boxed for his regiment in the Army. Tom was expected to use those skills in the interests of his younger brothers and sisters. Although not aggressive in character, his athletic abilities meant he was a naturally good boxer. It was something his siblings were only too aware of and they sometimes took advantage of it, which

Figure 0

led him into several street fights on their behalf. His advice to me, in my early secondary school years, was *"if set upon by several others, hit the biggest first with an uppercut to the chin, their legs will turn to jelly – the others will then run away"*. (I remembered this advice in my second year at Grammar School when someone chose to punch me for no reason. He lost two front teeth and I was never bothered again)

The Goodman family suffered considerable hardship leading up to the Great Depression of 1930. Thomas senior, my Grandfather, had retired from The Royal Artillery in 1929 and he found it difficult to find work in 'civvy street'. Bricklaying was his recorded line of work on the indenture forms that were completed as he joined the Army in 1905. His retirement gratuity of £20 did not last very long in keeping the Goodman family housed, fed and watered.

So, it was on 2nd September 1929 that Tom, then aged 15, decided to join the Army himself. (Fig 1) shows him proudly wearing his new uniform, on on the day that he joined up. He is pictured together with his best friend, Harry Rohl, who also appears in the photos of Tom's wedding taken in February 1940. What happened to Tom's relationship with Harry (Stanley?) Rohl after the wedding and World War 2 (WW2) is uncertain. However, it is possible that Harry emigrated to Auckland New Zealand after WW2 and died there aged 51, in February 1966.

The photo at (Fig 1) was taken in the back yard of the Goodman family home at 85, Thames Street, Greenwich. Not long after it was taken Thames Street was demolished and the Goodman family moved to the Honor Oak Estate. As may be observed, their Thames Street accommodation was of a poor standard. Tom joined the Army, in his own words, *"....to escape sleeping in a bed with my three younger brothers, in a bedroom where the roof leaked, for clean clothes, to gain an education, to have three hot meals a day and to earn some money to send home to help my Father, Mother and the rest of the family"*.

Figure 1

Tom was a bright and industrious boy and his school reference provided for the Army states *"Thomas Goodman has attended this school (Randall Place, LCC (B) School, Greenwich) for a number of years. During this period his conduct and attendance have been satisfactory. He is a keen intelligent lad who has carried out successfully the many duties that have been entrusted to him.*

H.E Bevans ,Class Teacher"

Industrious Tom had actually been offered a place at a Grammar school. However, there was a desperate lack of money in the Goodman household in 1929, there being no proper 'bread winner'. Tom's mother was *"taking in washing"* to try and keep the family fed. There was no money to buy Tom either a school uniform or the necessary books for going to a Grammar School. So, he had to forego that opportunity to further his thirst for learning and betterment. I know that this was a source of great disappointment for Tom and he long believed it had curtailed the breadth of opportunities open to him during his lifetime. However, he fully understood the reason why this decision was taken as he had endured the poverty at home first hand. Yet, his thirst for knowledge and its application for his personal improvement was never far from the surface. Given his own life experience, Tom always encouraged his own children to take every opportunity to further their education whenever they had the chance. He would have supported each of us without complaint for the sacrifices that he might have to make himself to enable our further education to take place. I, for one, can say we didn't always take his sound advice.

On joining up, Thomas John Goodman (Army No 1868344) was posted for training to the Royal Engineers (R.E) School of Electric Lighting, Gosport, where he served as a 'Boy Apprentice Tradesman, Turner' and began to study for his Army education exams. Given the opportunity to improve his education and future prospects, he passed the 2nd Class Army Education Certificate in November 1929. There he turned, as his first 'exam piece', a pair of wooden candle sticks that today adorn my dining table.

Figure 2

(Fig 2)

In August 1932, Tom was en-listed into the Training Battalion R.E. at Chatham for 'Recruit Training' and then was *posted to The Ranks*", a Sapper, on his 18th birthday, the 4th December 1932.

Aside from boxing, Tom proved to be a good athlete, swimmer and rugby player and was a successful sportsman at an early stage of his army career. His was No 3 Section, 22nd Company, The Royal Engineers, who were 1932 Athletic Champions and 1933 Winter Games Champions. (Fig 3) Tom is ID'd by his own 'tick' and is standing behind the Officers in row 3, 5th from the right.

Figure 3

June 1933 saw him join the 1st Anti-Aircraft Searchlight Battalion at Blackdown, Surrey, for 'A.A Duties, Workshops and Repair Party'.

Tom then embarked H.T. Remala (a Heavy Transport ship) for passage to the 16th Fortress Company, Malta, in September 1934. At Malta's Army Training centre he passed his 1st Class Army Education certificate in May 1935, which then equated to the 'Schools Certificate'. Tom had also made his second 'exam piece' a steel screw jack, that I also have for safe keeping. (Fig 4)

Figure 4

By June 1938, Tom had become "Instructor I/C of the Drawing Office", as he had developed a flair for Technical Drawing and also passed his Army exams in that subject. In all, he spent the 4½ years on Malta employed on defence installations and reconstruction works. Several photographs exist of his time there and one enigmatic girl often appears in them. The sight of these photos always prompted a wry comment from my mother to the effect that, " .it was probably where he lost his hair" ! Although no other details are known, he had "happy times" in Malta according to my mother whom he had not yet met at that time. A postcard found in his document case shows he had spent some time at Ghajn Tuffieha (Fig 5). That is a bay, on the North West of the Island, where there was an

Army recreation camp. Ghajn Tuffieha is now quite developed and includes a campsite for Scouts. It is almost unrecognisable compared to the scene on his post card.

Figure 5

Amongst Tom's documents there were some items that proved he had been a founder member, and Scoutmaster, of Malta's Lyceum II Scout troop. In his own words it was, *"..a troop for boys to help them learn some useful life skills and find the right way in the World"*. That was a sentiment which reflected his own childhood short comings and what he would have wished for himself. The boys of this troop were drawn from the only Maltese state Grammar School at that time. It was an early opportunity that he did not have for himself. Tom is seated in the centre. (Fig 6)

Figure 6

When Margaret and I were visiting Malta, in October 2000, we took a copy of Tom's Scoutmaster's Certificate dated 30th April 1937 and some of his scout troop photographs to the Scouting Headquarters in Valletta. (Fig 7)

By chance, we met the Chief Commissioner, Joe Grech. He welcomed us with open arms and we were invited to visit the nearby Island of Gozo with him, where the Certificate and Troop photo were incorporated into their Scouting Museum. After a cordial tour of the Museum, at

Figure 7

Triq Santa Dminka, in Victoria, we duly signed the visitors book and were then treated to lunch in a local fish restaurant by Joe Grech, Chief Commissioner. Joe was well known to the patron and other members of the clientele.

Whilst stationed in Malta, Tom had paraded several times on the Floriana parade ground to celebrate King George V's Birthday. A photograph inscribed in his own hand *"King's Birthday 1937"*, shows the Floriana parade ground packed with British troops marching in formation that mirrors Trooping The Colour ceremony we see performed annually on Horse Guards Parade, in Whitehall, London. Tom is believed to be marching proudly amongst the Ranks, somewhere on the Floriana parade ground in (Fig 8).Today, the Floriana parade ground has a hockey club, football pitches, Government offices and a large car park built upon it. It is known now as *Independence Ground*. However, the residential buildings, with covered balconies seen in the distance in (Fig 8) are still there, on the south west end of the square, along Vincenzo Dimech Road.

Figure 8

Tom's quest to improve his education was further evidenced as he enrolled at the Royal Malta University of Malta in 1935/36 and took a course in Mathematics and Mechanics, Pure and Applied. Tom returned to the UK from Malta on 25th May 1938, arriving on HMS Dorsetshire, a County Class heavy cruiser of the Royal Navy.

HMS Dorsetshire was subsequently sunk in action with the enemy on 5th April 1942, near Colombo, Ceylon, now known as Sri Lanka.

Figure 9

I know that Tom's maternal Uncle, Sidney Goodman, met up with him in Valletta, when the Royal Navy ship Sidney was serving in visited the Island, not long before Tom was posted back to the UK

On his return to the UK, Tom joined *M. Company R.E* and enrolled on No 13 (Electrical & Mechanical) Class at the School of Mechanical Engineering, Chatham. On 3rd September 1938 he was appointed *'acting, unpaid, Lance Corporal' with M Coy R.E.'* Then, on 20th September 1938, he was posted to 1st AA Battalion R.E. and reverted to *Sapper,* having sought permission to leave "The Colours" early, under Kings Regs 382(ii)(a)(i). This paragraph in the King's regulations provides for a solider to be released early from his signed up term, viz. : '*To enable a soldier to transfer to the reserve within 3 months of the end of his service to take up 'civil employment, which cannot be held open'*. On 9th October 1938, Tom left the army and was consequently transferred onto the British Army's Reserve. It is believed that Tom had decided to leave in 1938 because he could not progress out of "The Ranks" and also because he had then met his future wife, Ivy Kathleen Waters. (Fig 9). I suspect he was also disgruntled about the *'unpaid'* promotion.

The job Tom took in "Civvy Street" was working to the Chief Inspector of Armaments at Woolwich Arsenal, London. In that role, he was involved in *"the design of shells, Aircraft Bombs, Jigs, Gauges and the compilation of technical Instructions for the inspection of these items"*. This experience would later prove to have a significant influence on the path his Army career would take. He also sought to further his education at the South East London Technical College in 1938, by enrolling on a Senior Mechanical Engineering course. He was exempt the first year and came 2nd in class, in the second year's exams. Had he been able to complete that course it would have qualified him to apply for a commission, through natural progression.

However, the growing hostilities in Europe put paid to Tom completing the third and final year of that Engineering course, because he was recalled from the Army Reserve before the final examination could be taken. On 15th June 1939, he was '*called up for service*' and posted to join 'H.Q. Wing 1st Anti-Aircraft Battalion, Royal Engineers', at

Blackdown "*to train the Militia*". The 1st A.A. Battalion RE was a regular unit originally formed in 1922.

On 18th August 1939 Tom was '*Relegated to Army Reserve*'. Why is not explained. Perhaps it was due the fluctuating political situation leading up to World War 2 and the military's organisational preparations which were then in hand in the light of the worsening situation in Europe and the inevitable need for a General Mobilisation of the U.K.'s defence forces, against the increasing threat of hostilities with Nazi Germany. He returned on leave to his new parental home at No 12, Curlew House on the Honor Oak Estate, Brockley, SE.

Close to where the Waters family lived at 3 Holdenby Road, Crofton Park, London SE4 is The Rivoli Ballroom. It is quite possible that Tom met my mother, Ivy, there. I know they used to frequent The Rivoli before and after they met. The Rivoli has been through several transformations in its history. Most recently it was used as a location in the BBC's 2023 series "*We Hunt Together*" and is noted for its splendid 1950's red velvet interior decor. (Fig 10)

Figure 10

Under the command chain of 2 AA Brigade, the 1st AA Battalion RE, commanded by Lt-Col R.M. Goldney RA, was ordered to mobilise on 1st September 1939.

War with Germany was declared two days later.

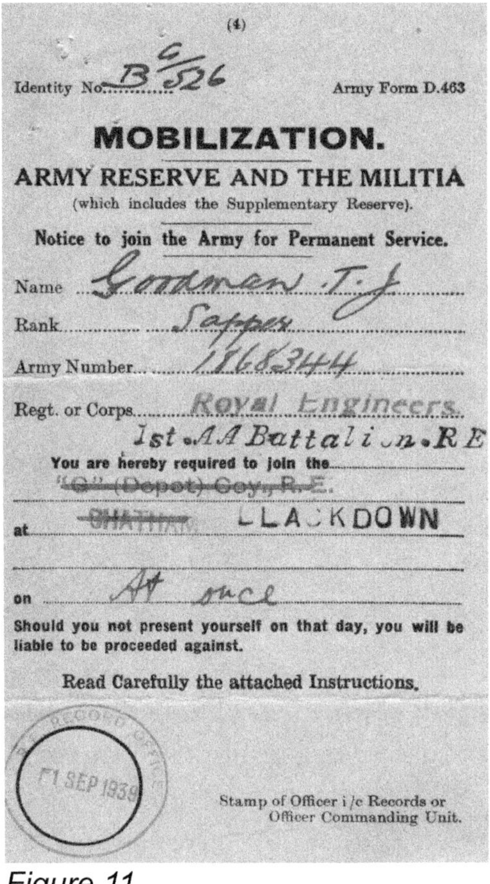

(4)

Identity No. G/B 526 Army Form D.463

MOBILIZATION.

ARMY RESERVE AND THE MILITIA

(which includes the Supplementary Reserve).

Notice to join the Army for Permanent Service.

Name Goodman T.J

Rank Sapper

Army Number 1868344

Regt. or Corps Royal Engineers

1st AA Battalion RE

You are hereby required to join the ~~"G" (Depot) Coy., R.E.~~

at ~~CHATHAM~~ BLACKDOWN

on At once

Should you not present yourself on that day, you will be liable to be proceeded against.

Read Carefully the attached Instructions.

RECORD OFFICE 1 SEP 1939

Stamp of Officer i/c Records or Officer Commanding Unit.

Figure 11

Tom's '*Urgent Mobilisation*' for World War 2 arrived at Curlew House on 2nd September 1939 and he was '*instructed to report at once to Blackdown, 1st A.A. Battalion R.E.*" (Fig11) Back at Blackdown Camp, where Tom had previously been stationed, he was involved with making hurried preparations with his Anti-Aircraft Searchlight unit in advance of embarking for France with the British Expeditionary Force (B.E.F.). Blackdown Camp was located near to Camberley, in Surrey. It was established in the early 1900s when the Royal Engineers built barracks there at a number of locations. It remained in use by successive branches of the Army until, in 2008, it was finally decided to progressively sell off the land for new housing and it was fully decommissioned in 2021.

Chapter 2 - B.E.F Dunkirk

The R.E. A.A. Battalion Head Quarters' 1 and 2 Batteries main contingent left Blackdown and embarked at Southampton on 10th September 1939. They landed at Cherbourg Naval Base, France, the following day. It would seem that the deployment of the 1st A.A. Bn R.E. is likely to have been an error, as it is alleged in several authoritative tomes, that the movement order was supposed to have said *'less 1st A.A. Bn RE'* - as that battalion was originally intended to be deployed to defend the Thames Estuary !

Several Thames Estuary defences were planned, including one at Shivering Sands. This was an Army defensive position, a Maunsell Fort, built near the Thames estuary

Figure 12

for anti-aircraft defence (Fig12). The towers were built on dry land and then floated out into position in 1943. It was made up of six interconnected towers and located off Herne Bay, in Kent, and is 9.2 miles north of there, which is the closest point of land. On clear days, the structures can still be viewed from the coast.

The Shivering Sands fort was the last of the Thames estuary forts to be constructed, and was progressively installed between 18 September and 13 December 1943.

The Anti-Aircraft Search Light installation is just visible on the middle of the 5 remaining Anti-Aircraft gun emplacement structures in (Fig 13).

Just 10 days after his "Mobilization", on 12th September 1939, Sapper Tom Goodman was on his way 'Overseas' with the British Expeditionary Force (B.E.F.) to France, with the 1st Anti-Aircraft Searchlight Battalion, R.E. (Order of Battle 1AA Group).

Figure 13

Tom's service record shows that he actually landed in France, at Brest.(Fig 14-1). It was some considerable distance from the actual fighting front and, being rather unprepared for action, the British army's various elements probably needed time to organise themselves on the ground and for transport.

Figure 14

Also, the B.E.F.'s westerly route across the channel to Brest was less likely to be subject to attack from the Luftwaffe than if it took the shortest crossing to France via Dover-Calais.

In 1938, it was decided that the Royal Engineer (R.E.) AA Units would join the Royal Artillery (R.A.). In the case of 1 AA Battalion R.E. this did not happen until around January 1940, when it was redesignated 1 Searchlight Regiment R.A., along with 2, 3 and 4 Searchlight Batteries R.A. The R.A. Regimental History notes that, during the B.E.F's campaign, 1 and 2 Batteries were actually R.E. while 3 and 4 were R.A.

On arrival in France, the main Battalion was deployed to protect the B.E.F.'s No 2 Base Sub-area at Nantes, but at the end of the month it moved up to Fauquembergues, where its searchlights cooperated with the night fighters of No 60 Wing, Royal Air Force in the Aircraft Fighting Zone (AFZ) bounded by Bergues, Cassel and Guisnes (just inland from the ports of Boulogne, Calais and Dunkirk). The 72-

light Searchlights were laid out, with an average separation of 4500 yards, seven rows deep, with Mk VIII Sound locators in the first row and was built up from west to east as 3rd Searchlight Battery arrived. The 3rd Searchlight Battery, R.A. had mobilised at Portsmouth, and sailed from Southampton disembarking on 16th September at Brest, where it was delayed for a week awaiting the arrival of much of its transport – another indication of the lack of preparedness. It joined the rest of the battalion on 3rd October and deployed three days later. On 17th October the battalion came under the command of 2nd AA Brigade, and on 2nd November the first Luftwaffe raider came over the battalion's area and a Heinkel He 111 was shot down by the R.A.F.

The 4th Searchlight Battery, RA, mobilised on 1st December at Yeovil and sailed from Southampton to Cherbourg on 8th December 1939. It joined the Battalion and began deploying round La Capelle-lès-Boulogne on 21st December, filling in the western end of the AFZ. This brought the number of lights operated by the battalion up to 96. From late December 1939, the regiment provided two sections at Boulogne and Dunkirk to cooperate with Light Anti Aircraft (LAA) guns in trying to prevent German seaplanes from dropping parachute mines into their harbours.

The 1st Anti-Aircraft Searchlight Battalion R.E., which included Tom, was disbanded in January 1940 when the 1st Searchlight Regiment R.A. was formed by combining other Searchlight units and transferring personnel in from the Infantry and the Royal Engineers. Tom had elected to stay within the Royal Engineers, as did a number of the Officers.

However, they remained on the strength of the Searchlight Regiment until they were able to be *'Taken on the Strength'* of another R.E. unit. In practice, this would not happen until after they returned to the UK.

Tom's record shows he was granted *"10 days leave in UK to marry Ivy Kathleen Waters* (my mother) *in Lewisham"*. (Fig 15).They were married on 10th February 1940, at St Hilda's Church in Brockley Rise, Crofton Park, London, SE4.

Tom returned to France, to re-join B.E.F., ten days later on 20th February 1940.

Figure 15

Wondering again about how my parents came to meet, it's interesting to note that my mother's youngest brother, Robert (Rob) Waters, was also a member of the Royal Engineers and from the photographic evidence to hand, he was also the member of an R.E. Anti-

Aircraft Searchlight Battery. Rob is second from the right in (Fig 16).

Tom's service record also states that he again *"returned to the UK on leave"* on 20th March 1940, before returning to France for a second time on 9th April 1940 where he rejoined *'1st Searchlight Battalion R.E. B.E.F.'*

Another member of the Royal Engineers was Fredrick Charles Burley (a Heavy Turner) who subsequently married my father's eldest sister, Winifred.

Figure 16

On the 10th May 1940, Tom's Regiment was deployed around Lille (Fig 14-2), under 5 AA Brigade, which was the General Headquarters of the B.E.F.

By 16th May 1940, the Regimental HQ was ordered to send 1, 3 and 4 AA Batteries to secure the bridges over the canal from Bethune to La Brassee, while 2 AA Battery moved to Arras (Fig 14-3) to build road blocks around the town. Between 17th and 19th May 1940, 1 and 2 AA Batteries were sent to Calais (Fig 14-4) where they came under the command of HQ British Troops Calais, Colonel RT Holland DSO, MC. They were based in Fort Risban and Fort Vert in the town of Calais, close to the harbour. They were to be secured because Calais was intended to become a main supply port to the British Expeditionary Force.

At Calais, both 1 and 2 AA Batteries were used in a dual searchlight / infantry role and the soldiers were used to establish roadblocks around Calais. Searchlight troops made first contact with German panzer troops on 23rd May at Les Attaques, which may have played a part in convincing the Germans that Calais was strongly held, although at that date it certainly was not. Once H.Q. 30 Infantry Brigade arrived on 22nd May 1940, under Brigadier C. N. Nicholson, both batteries came under his command.

Airey Neave M.P. was a Subaltern (Lieutenant) in No 1 Battery Royal Artillery. He was wounded and captured at Calais. He subsequently achieved fame for his escape activity at the P.O.W. camp Colditz and through his post war political career. In 1979, he was assassinated by the Irish Republican Army, who placed a bomb under his car. It exploded as he left the underground car park at The Houses of Parliament, Westminster. I wonder if Tom and Airey Neave ever met ?

No 3 and 4 AA Batteries were relieved on the canal by 20th May and sent to Hazebrouck area under command of 2 AA Brigade, to defend the town. They were ordered to withdraw from Hazebrouck on 24 May and their places were taken by the 46th Infantry Division (Polforce). They withdrew to Dunkirk and were deployed to hold part of the canal line near Bergues (towards Hondschoote). They were relieved on 28th May 1940 and ordered to destroy all vehicles and equipment. They were evacuated from the Dunkirk beaches that night.

Figure 17

Both 1 and 2 A.A. Batteries fought as infantry in the Battle of Calais until they were forced to surrender on 26 May 1940. (featured in the film "Darkest Hour"). However, the regimental records indicate that a small detachment of them escaped from Calais and made their way up to the beaches of Dunkirk - "every man for himself". (Fig 17). Not having been taken a prisoner of War, my Father (Tom) must have been amongst that small detachment to escape from Calais and his recollection of the action confirms that. His Army record details him back in England and joining 'M Company, No 1 Depot Battalion, R.E., ex B.E.F. on 23rd June 1940'. The date of my Father's return from France indicates that he was amongst the last to leave Dunkirk.

The B.E.F. rescue operation was called *Operation Dynamo* (Fig 18) and included the famous fleet of 'Small Ships' that assisted with the evacuation from the beaches. Tom spoke briefly, on just a couple of occasions, about his experience in the B.E.F theatre of War.

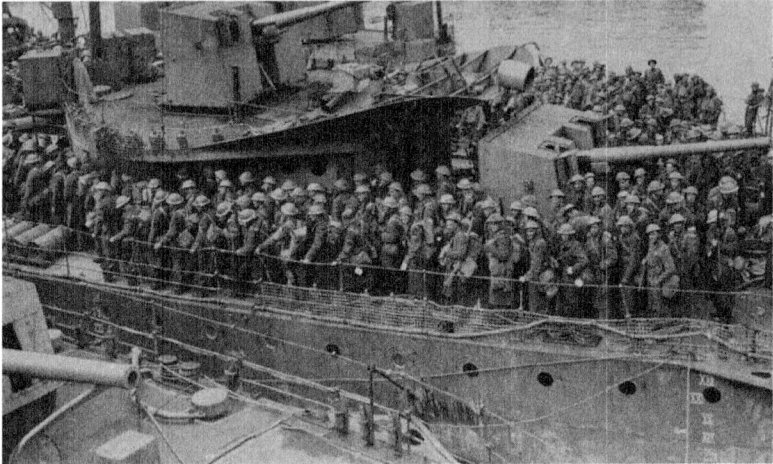

Figure 18

He was certainly not impressed by the outdated World War 1 tactics employed by the British Generals to fight a heavily mechanised modern German Army. He did not have a good word to say about the way British forces had been so poorly equipped and prepared when he was first deployed into France. It was also apparent that he had been involved in helping to render unserviceable the mass of vehicles, artillery and other equipment being left behind on the retreat to the Dunkirk beaches, in the face of the advancing German army. Amongst other things, he had walked the lines of abandoned vehicles, removing electrical components, draining oil from their sumps and running their engines to make them seize up. He had also removed essential parts from artillery equipment when they ran out of the explosive charges and hand grenades that they had been using to disable them. (Fig 19)

Figure 19

Tom's experiences with the B.E.F. certainly made him determined to try and take charge of his own destiny, as far as possible that is, for the remainder of the hostilities.

In 1953, The 1940 Dunkirk Veterans' Association (D.V.A.) was formed. It was an association of British service veterans "...*who served at Dunkirk and other ports of evacuation between 10 May and June 1940*" – that is in the Dunkirk evacuation of 1940, including those who were taken prisoner from the beaches. Associate membership was available to those "… *otherwise not qualified, but who had assisted at the ports of evacuation*".

Five veterans who had been on the Dunkirk Beach or in the vicinity fighting, met in the bar of the Queens Hotel, City Square, Leeds on 3 September 1953. They wanted to foster the spirit of comradeship and support experienced during the evacuation and support fellow veterans who had fallen on hard times. The first membership card, no 1, showed the 6d subscription collected and receipted by Harold Robinson (he was awarded an MBE in 1970 for services to veterans charities) who had been voted in as Honorary General Secretary and stayed in that honorary post until his death in 1988, whilst working as a schoolteacher.

The Association started to arrange pilgrimages to the beaches and towns from which troops had been evacuated including Dunkirk, De Panne, Bray Dunes and Calais. During the first pilgrimage, by 45 veterans in 1954, they realised that the local towns and population were still suffering deprivation and shortages. Subsequently, D.V.A. members arranged food parcels for the local population. As the D.V.A. expanded more veterans joined the pilgrimages. The accepted rule was you paid your own way there and joined fellow veterans at pre-booked Hotel and B&B accommodation. Some stayed with families they had met during the evacuation who had assisted them, taking the opportunity to repay kindnesses. These pilgrimages took place when large parts of the towns and villages were still exhibiting severe War damage and rebuilding had not fully started.

Remembrance services were held on beaches, villages and towns, many conducted by the Reverend Leslie Aitken (later Right Rev. and MBE) who was the D.V.A's. first and only

'Padre' having been part of the founding group. Aitken was the author of *Massacre on the road to Dunkirk*, detailing the murder by an SS company of 45 officers and men at Wormhoudt, in France.

In 1956 Queen Elizabeth, The Queen Mother, agreed to be their patron and attended the 1957 pilgrimage unveiling the Dunkirk Memorial and taking the salute at a march past of D.V.A. of members in the Place de Jean Bart in Dunkirk, where over 1000 veterans paraded. At its peak membership in the mid 1970s, over 20,000 veterans from the UK, with increasing numbers of expatriates and Commonwealth Dunkirk Veterans, would make the pilgrimage trip each year to honour their fallen comrades.

Figure 20

The Dunkirk Medal (*Medaille Dunkerque 1940*) is an unofficial commemorative medal created by the town of Dunkirk to commemorate the defence of the town and surrounding area during May and June 1940. The allocation of the award was managed by *Nationale des Anciens Combattants de Flandres-Dunkerque 1940*, the French National Association of Veterans of the Fortified Sector of Flanders and Dunkirk. (Fig 20.)

Initiated in 1960, the Dunkirk Medal was, at first, only awarded to French service personnel (with approximately

30,000 medals issued). In 1970 it was also awarded to any Allied member involved in Operation Dynamo, the evacuation of Allied forces from the Dunkirk sector between 29 May and 3 June and those soldiers evacuated from the beaches. All British servicemen from the Army, Royal Navy, Royal Air Force, Merchant Navy, and the civilian little ship volunteers were eligible to receive the award. It was later administered in the UK by the Dunkirk Veterans Association (D.V.A.), which was disbanded in 2000 because natural attrition had greatly reduced the membership.

Tom would have known about this 'unofficial' award as, at the time, it was widely reported in military circles and the national press. For reasons known only to himself, he did not come forward to claim it. I actually believe that his modesty had prevailed. Having discovered his eligibility, I researched the D.V.A. and, with a lead from Poppy Research, wrote directly to the Mayor of Dunkirk in early 2021, including a copy of Tom's service record. After a timely exchange of correspondence, a commemorative "Coup" and the following letter (translated verbatim via Google) arrived in August 2022.

"Sir,

You were kind enough to inform us of the participation of your father - a British soldier, in the battles of Dunkirk and you are asking us for the possibility of obtaining the commemorative medal linked to this event. Unfortunately, the Marine Dunkerque association responsible for awarding this medal dissolved in the year 2000 and we are therefore unable to respond to your request. However, to respond to your wish to honour the memory of your father, we can send

you the dish created during the ceremonies organized for the 70th Anniversary of the Battle of Dunkirk and Operation Dynamo in our city. Also, thank you for giving us your postal address so that we can send it to you by post.
Please accept, Sir, the expression of our best feelings.
Fabrice Baert,
Special Advisor to the Mayor for Military Affairs and Veterans Affairs"

The silver dish (Coupe) that arrived is shown at (Fig 21).

So, contrary to the popular press, the *entente cordiale* appears to have survived.

After his return from Dunkirk, Tom was posted to *"D Company No3 (Lines of Communication) Depot Battalion R.E.'* at the School of Military Engineering, Chatham, and was promoted

Figure 21

to *"Acting / Staff Sergeant"* with effect from 22nd June 1940. Shortly afterwards, on 11th July 1940, he was posted to Newark in Lincolnshire, to join No2 Mechanical Equipment Training Company R.E. as *'Instructor and Military Machinist I/C of the Workshops, Installation of Machinery, Maintenance of Plant'* and promoted to Staff Sergeant. There followed a further promotion to Master Staff Sergeant on 22nd September 1940, this time each promotion was remunerated.

Coincident with this posting, the newly weds took billeted accommodation in Spalding, Lincolnshire. I know, for sure, that my mother was not very happy living there. It was the first time she had lived away from her parental home. Being the youngest of the Waters brood, my mother missed her family in Crofton Park and with Tom working miles away at the Depot, in Newark she would have been alone for a lot of the time. Their Spalding accommodation was a one room bed sit and not at all what Ivy had been used to at her parental home at 3, Holdenby Road, Crofton Park, London. So, it was not very long before Ivy moved

Figure 22

back to live at her family home in Crofton Park (Fig 22). I also know that Ivy's early cooking skills were somewhat "basic". I have overheard several recollections about "*burnt stew dinners*" that Ivy produced on a Baby Belling stove (an electric ring) in their bed-sit. However, in early 1941 there came the opportunity came along for Tom and Ivy to rent a, first floor, three bedroom flat at 35a Holdenby Road, SE4 (Fig 23).

Figure 23

It was an ideal location, being just a few doors up the road from the Waters' family home at No 3. Tom and Ivy retained that flat until 1966, despite being abroad for several years on foreign postings with the Army after the War ended. In the early 1960s, as a family, we visited Spalding and the couple that Tom and Ivy had been billeted with during WW2. We were made most welcome by them. The then elderly couple were referred to as *"Granny and Grandad Spalding"* and we had afternoon tea with them. I still have the china WW1 tank I was allowed to select from their *Goss* collection which was proudly displayed in a large glass cabinet of many such pieces, in their lounge.(Fig 24). As far as I know that was the last time they met up with *"The Spaldings"*, but there was an exchange of Christmas cards for several years after that visit.

Figure 24

The flat at 35a Holdenby Road did not have its own air raid shelter. Instead, Ivy used to make her way down to her parents house at No3, where they had a Morrison Shelter installed. This was the version of air raid shelter that could also be used as a table (Fig 25). About half a million of the kits had been distributed by the government, by December 1941. It was "free issue" to households that had an income of less than £400 a year. As the house at No 3 was one of the few privately owned houses in Holdenby Road (most were rental properties like 35a) it is unlikely they received a "free issue". My maternal Grandfather was a skilled mechanical engineer who worked for a firm at the Limb Fitting Centre, Roehampton Hospital. He had invented the first articulated false arm in the post WW1 period. This was quite a contentious matter in the Waters family, as he believed that he had not received full recognition of his contribution by the Company. The "Morrison" shelter must have been most the uncomfortable, and cramped, of air raid shelters. I know that my mother decided to stop using it after a short while. She didn't even go back to using it after my elder brother was born, in 1942, which might have been a more eventful decision had lady luck not have been on her side.

In 1943 many thousands more Morrisons were issued in response to the German's newly deployed V1 (doodlebug) attacks.

Figure 25

Chapter 3 - Bomb Disposal Years

As the war progressed, it became apparent that unexploded bombs (UXBs) were equally disruptive to the War effort as those that went bang. This was highlighted by the Blitz which resulted in many areas of London being evacuated and cordoned off because of UXBs. So, in September 1939, it was decided by the War Office that the Royal Engineers (R.E.) would provide temporary Bomb Disposal (B.D.) teams, until the Home Office could recruit and train special Air Raid Precaution teams to undertake the role. However, it was soon realised that this arrangement would not work.

Figure 26

The *Formation Order* of May 1940 formally handed responsibility for Bomb Disposal to the Royal Engineers and 25 Bomb Disposal sections were created. B.D. demand was so great that this was soon increased to 134 sections. The original bomb disposal working parties were absorbed within the new organisation. In 1940, Queen Mary designed an arm badge to identify B.D. personnel who were active during the Blitz. (Fig 26)

The first R.E. B.D. teams consisted of a Non Commissioned Officer (NCO) and two sappers, who were required to dig down to the bombs and blow them up in situ. The first bombs to be dropped on the UK were in the Orkneys in October 1939, while the first unexploded bombs fell on the Shetlands in November 1939.

It was one thing to authorise the formation of units, but it was another to find the men, equipment and transport, all of which were in short supply. The sections were issued with standard R.E. stores such as hammers, chisels, blocks and tackles, picks and shovels plus a small amount of explosive. Bespoke B.D. equipment was still almost non-existent.

For the first few months, the bomb disposal units dug down to the bombs, using what shoring materials were available, often timber and doors from bomb damaged houses, corrugated iron, anything, in fact, they could lay their hands on. When they got down to the fuze, the officer would use a hammer and cold chisel to unscrew the locking ring, often withdrawing the fuze by hand or by tying a piece of string round the fuze boss which enabled him to do it by remote control. The bomb was usually rolled over to empty the fuze pocket of the picrics (the primary explosive charge), then loaded on a truck and taken to a dump. In those days a 'truck' would not have been an army issue but anything from an 'impressed' van through to a cattle truck or, if you were lucky, a normal lorry of the time. Despite almost non-existent equipment and very little training, the sections learnt fast. In June 1940, just 20 unexploded bombs were dealt with. This rose to 100 in July, 300 in August and over 3,000 in September 1940. By this point, the B.D. sections had increased in number again and been organised into 25 B.D. Companies. Between September 1940 and July 1941, over 24,000 bombs were made safe and removed. In 1942 and

1944, B.D. Companies also joined the task forces for the invasions of Malta and France.

In the event, the original B.D. organisation was unworkable. Although belonging to the Corps of Royal Engineers, they were 'War Office' controlled by a department called the *Inspector of Fortifications,* headed by a Royal Artillery General. Fortunately, the Minister of Supply formed an Unexploded Bomb Committee, whose purpose was to consider all problems relative to bomb disposal.

The relative sizes of German bombs are shown at (Fig 27).

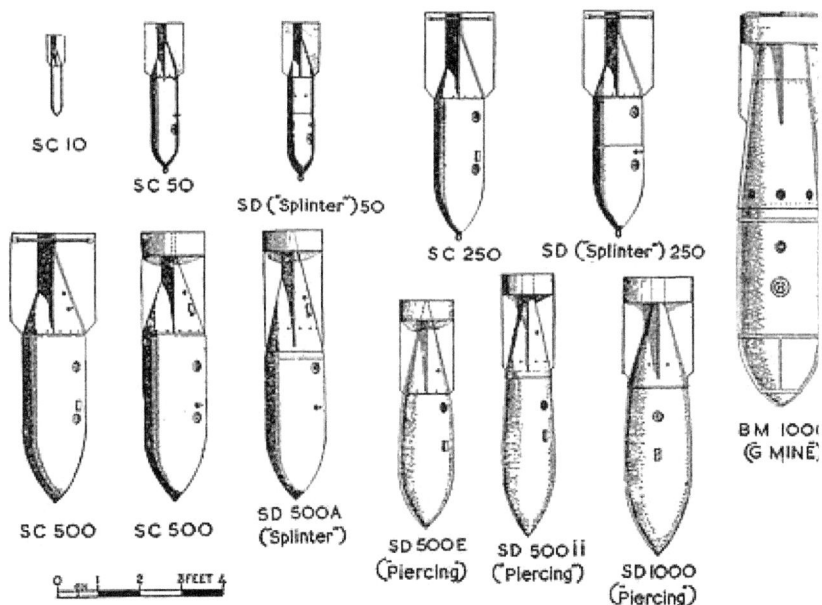

SC 10

SC 50

SD ('Splinter')50

SC 250   SD ('Splinter') 250

SC 500   SC 500   SD 500A
('Splinter')

SD 500E   SD 500ii
(Piercing)   (Piercing)   SD 1000
(Piercing)

BM 1000
(G MINE)

Figure 27

By the end of June 1940 it came apparent that the twenty five B.D. Companies already formed would, in no way, be able to cope with the expected deluge of bombs that would result from the withdrawal of our forces through Dunkirk and elsewhere. Another 109 B.D. Companies were authorised. Volunteers were called for and a few came forward. In the main the Other Ranks were just 'posted in'. Most of the young officers came straight from a Royal Engineers Officer Cadet Training Unit (O.C.T.U.). Some had received an immediate commission as a result of their technical or professional qualifications. All ranks were informed that they could, after six months service in bomb disposal, elect to transfer to another branch of the Royal Engineers. This offer was made because it was thought that the strain would be too much. Very few took up the offer and many served with distinction throughout the whole of the war. Up to the end of July 1940, bombing had still been light and the sections had been coping with the volume, if not the different new fuzes which were appearing and causing many B.D. team deaths. It was agreed that there should be a better organisation, with support and control of the Independent sections. These were now 220 in number and they were formed into companies, each of ten sections plus a company headquarters. The Gunner General was replaced by a Sapper, Major General G.B.O.Taylor and the department was renamed *Inspector of Fortifications and Director of Bomb Disposal*. This change took place on 29th August 1940 - the very day that the Luftwaffe started its blitz offensive on London.

The Blitz was to prove almost too much for the newly formed and poorly trained B.D. sections, who were at the receiving end of the unprecedented scale of bombing, never experienced before by any civilian population.

It was on 31st January 1941 that Staff Sergeant Goodman received orders to proceed (with driver P Wolley) for interview by Colonel W Garforth D.S.O. M.C. R.E., staff officer to the Chief Engineer, Northern Command in York. The result of that interview was Tom's appointment to a Commission (in the R.E. Officer Corps) and promotion to *Lieutenant* with effect from 1st March 1941. (Fig 28)

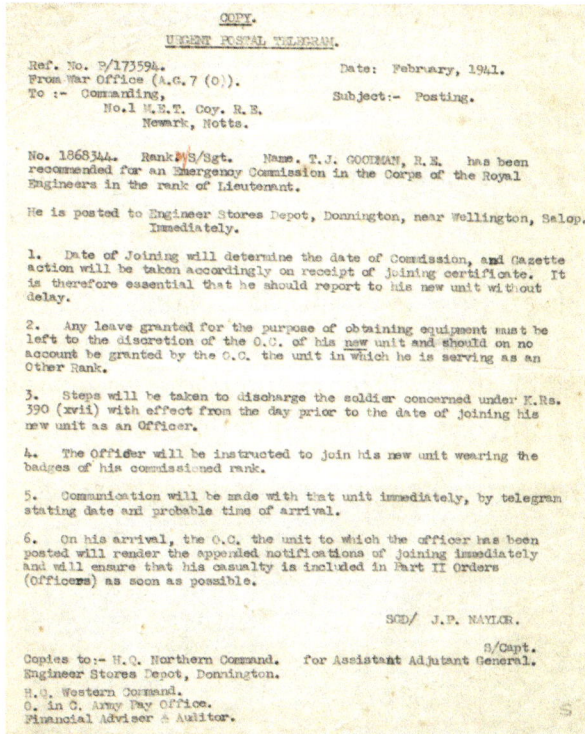

Figure 28

Tom was now a Royal Engineers Bomb Disposal (B.D.) Officer.

His promotion was published in the Supplement to The London Gazette on 28th March 1941 and he was then assigned a new Army number, P173594, which replaced his original army number, 1868344, that had been allocated on his joining 'The Ranks' in 1929. (Fig 29)

1786   SUPPLEMENT TO THE LONDON GAZETTE, 28 MARCH, 1941

26th Feb. 1941:—
    Serjt. Douglas Edward APTED (173550).
27th Feb. 1941:—
    M.Q.M.S. Frank Weston GEE (175157).
28th Feb. 1941:—
    M.Q.M.S. Edward George RATHBONE (175167).
    B.S.M. Hugh SIDEBOTTOM (175156).
    Serjt. Ernest William Hepton BOND (175202).
1st Mar. 1941:—
    B.S.M. Arthur James SAGE (175161).
3rd Mar. 1941:—

27th Feb. 1941:—
    C.S.M. Percy FENSOME (173565).
    C.S.M. George BRANTINGHAM (173331).
28th Feb. 1941:—
    Q.M.S. Instr. Leslie Albert HARPER (173544).
    Corpl. Albert Donovan MARMONT (175182).
1st Mar. 1941:—
    Q.M.S. Instr. Thomas CLYDESDALE (173322).
    S. Serjt. Thomas John GOODMAN (173594).
5th Mar. 1941:—
    W.O. Cl. II Frank CARR (175626).

Figure 29

The photograph at (Fig 30) was taken during the blackout in WW2. The group are at my mother's family house, No 3 Holdenby Road, SE4. My Father (Tom) is in the Officer's uniform (rear 2nd right). It is highly likely that this was taken in 1941 soon after he was Commissioned. I do recall my Mother saying *"Tom came home on a short leave and hadn't told anyone about his promotion beforehand. He simply turned up on the doorstep and surprised us all with pips on his shoulders".* My guess is that this picture was taken on that occasion. I wonder if he told my mother that he had

Figure 30

42

volunteered to join Bomb Disposal (B.D.) to achieve his 'pips'

(Fig 30 L to R – Fredrick Burley, Winifred Goodman, Rob Waters, Alice Waters, Tom Goodman, Ivy Goodman (nee Waters)

Tom's first B.D. posting was to Donnington, Salop (Shropshire) as *"Stores Officer, Engineers Supply Central Depot"*.

Donnington's development from a greenfield site had begun in 1939. The site was chosen in 1936 as one of a number of less vulnerable locations for storing ordnance and other military equipment previously kept at London's Woolwich Arsenal. During 1940 the depot (Central Ordinance Depot) was established and at the end of the year Brigadier Charles Esmond de Wolff was appointed commandant and garrison commander. During 1941 and 1942 the depot increased significantly in size and, by the end of 1941, 9,600 all ranks worked on the site. Brigadier de Wolff also convinced Wellington District Council to build housing for the civilian staff, many of whom had moved up from Woolwich. Eventually, 1,500 houses were built outside the Depot.

Figure 31

Tom's stay at Donnington was to last a mere 4 weeks

and, as it was the Royal Engineers first formal bomb disposal school, Tom would have received his initial B.D. training there, acquiring the requisite background knowledge in connection with his next B.D. role. This was a posting to Long Marston, Warwickshire on 20th April 1941, where he assumed the role of 'Officer In Charge of Bomb Disposal Stores and Canadian Diamond Drilling'. (Fig 31)

The Bomb Disposal Stores were the focal point for the assembly, storage and distribution of the bespoke equipment that was developed to tackle the UXB problem. Examples of UXB types were gathered there to provide a training facility and for the development of defuzing equipment. A role that Tom was well suited to given his previous work during 1938 at The Woolwich Arsenal, where his record notes that he was engaged in "the design of shells, Aircraft Bombs, Jigs, Gauges and compilation of technical Instructions for the inspection of these items".

Figure 32

The first piece of equipment produced for the B.D. officer was the 'Crabtree' discharger. (Fig 32). It was a simple device with two spikes that connected to the electrical plungers on a fuze. When applied to a fuze, it discharged the electrical charge that had been applied to the fuze, in the bomb bay, just before it was dropped from the aircraft. It then rendered the trembler mechanism in the fuze harmless.

It also had a ring fitted to its top so that a piece of cord could be tied to it, allowing the B.D. Officer to extract the fuze from a safe distance. When the No 25 fuze was introduced, the two spikes were removed but the Crabtree was still used to extract the fuze.(Fig 33)

Figure 33

An essential piece of B.D. equipment was the 'Universal' fuze key. This consisted of a steel bar about twelve inches long with two adjustable lugs that could be fitted into the two slots of a locking ring. As soon as it was discovered that the locking rings were a standard fitting, and therefore no adjustment was needed, a much better fuze retaining ring key was designed with fixed lugs. (Fig 34)

Another piece of B.D. equipment was the *Steam Sterilizer*. Steam Sterilizing was necessary in situations where a UXB could not be manoeuvred to disarm the fuze, nor could it be detonated in situ, because of

Figure 34

the damage that would be caused to surrounding infrastructure. Its purpose was to circumvent the fuze and to allow emptying the bomb of its main explosive charge.

However, before it could be used it required either the base filling plate to be removed or for a hole to be cut in the bomb casing using a *Canadian Diamond Drill* (Fig 31). It was the only way for the B.D. Officer to circumvent a type 17 fuze, with a Zus 40 (anti-withdrawal) booby trap below it.

Both drilling and steaming activity could activate a fuze. However, they were used to great effect once the fuzes had been immunised, but their extraction might have resulted in the bomb exploding. In which case the contents were steamed out and the explosion caused by the setting off the fuze pocket(s) was relatively small and minimal surrounding damage was done.

The 'clock stopper' was a very substantial electrical coil that was placed on the casing around a bomb's fuze. It induced a strong magnetic field to stop the clockwork mechanism running and the ticking could be monitored by a stethoscope.

The Canadian Diamond drill is still used today to cut a hole in a bomb's outer casing. During the 'mid 1930s a civil war had been raging in Spain, and Germany was very much involved in it. This gave their airmen a lot of bombing practice and a chance to evaluate their bombs and fuzes. However little or no thought was given in the UK to Bomb Disposal at that time. Intelligence about the Spanish bombing campaign was common knowledge, in fact much information about their Bomb designs was available to anyone who cared to ask H.M. Stationery Office.

With the outbreak of WW2, the War Office recognised the need for a large engineer's depot and the 455 acre site adjacent to the station at Long Marston was selected for the construction of No.1 Royal Engineer's Supply Depot and

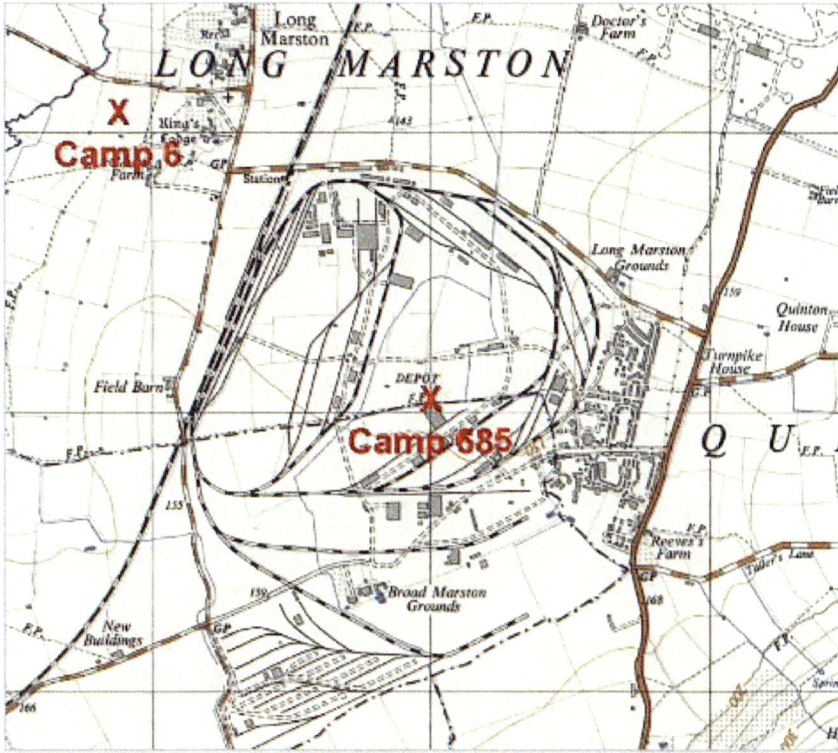

Figure 35

Long Marston Airfield.(Fig 35) The function of this Depot was to store resources for Army Engineers in a series of storage sheds and warehouses of varying sizes. Many of these were connected by rail and served by sidings off a main loop line which ran around the site. Besides the storage sheds and warehouses, the Long Marston camp consisted of smaller buildings of varying sizes including, timber and brick barracks and Nissen huts which housed the Royal Engineers looking after the stores. Towards the end of the war part of the camp was also used to house German POWs.

On a trip to the Isle of Wight, in 2010, I visited the Isle of Wight Steam Railway to ride on it from Havenstreet to Wooton. To my amazement, at Havenstreet station, I was confronted by the sight of a gleaming green steam locomotive in the shunting yard. It was the very loco' that I had ridden the footplate of at Long Marston, in 1964. (Fig 36). The loco' was named '*Royal Engineer*' (WD198) a 0-6-0 ST. Built for the War Office in 1953. WD198 did not enter service until 1956 when it worked at the General Stores Sub-Depot at Steventon. It then moved to Central Ordnance Depot, Bicester in 1958 and finally to HQ Engineer Resources at Long Marston in 1961. After Long Marston closed, there followed a long period in store before the loco was restored to working order and in 1971 was given the name Royal Engineer. A further overhaul followed in 1987/88 and, when it was withdrawn from service in 1991, it

Figure 36

48

was the last operational steam locomotive owned by the Army. *Royal Engineer* was part of a collection of railway items acquired by the Royal Corps of Transport Museum's Trust for eventual display at a new museum under development at Chatham. As an interim measure, *Royal Engineer* was placed on loan to the Isle of Wight Steam Railway and following the fitting of Westinghouse air brake equipment it was put to work on passenger services. In May 2008 the National Army Museum transferred the ownership to the Isle of Wight Steam Railway. *Royal Engineer* is currently in service on the line and as one of their most powerful locomotives she can haul the heaviest trains with ease.

Figure 37

In 1941, as part of the U.X.B. awareness campaign, a film entitled '*UXB*' was produced by the Army Kinematograph Service (Figs 37,38). It was shown on B.D. training courses to personnel in the Army, Navy, Civil Defence and Air Raid Precaution Warden briefings, to help them recognise the tell tale differences on the ground between a bomb that had exploded and one that was Unexploded (UXB).

Figure 38

49

One evening in 1973, without any clues, Tom asked me to watch a programme on the TV for him and to report back what it was about. He could not stay home to watch it himself, as he was committed to attending a meeting of The Chiswick House Residents Association that evening. There was no such thing as a domestic VCR or iPlayer in those days to enable viewing of television programmes after they had been broadcast "to air". I duly obliged. Three minutes into the programme (UXB film) there was pan shot across a mixed audience consisting of Military and Civilian representatives.

There in the middle of the group was Tom, with hand on chin, in his typical *"I'm thinking"* pose. I nearly fell off my chair ! (Fig 39)

Figure 39

On his return home that evening, I described what the film was about and he smiled wryly. Yes, he had seen film crews on several occasions when he was undertaking his B.D. briefing and training sessions at Donnington. However, he'd never actually seen the film himself either during WW2 or after and, to my knowledge, that 1941 'UXB' film was not repeated on TV again in his lifetime.

At the time, I asked my Tom why he chose to join Bomb Disposal. He replied, *"It had several advantages. After the Dunkirk shambles, I decided I would try and determine my own destiny by not being cannon fodder for the Generals, in so far as it is possible in War time. In Bomb Disposal, I could sleep in my own dry and comfy bed, enjoy the hospitality that was afforded to B.D. teams by the public when out on a job and I got the chance to nip home to see my new wife, now and then !"*

I believe that Tom volunteered for B.D. to gain his Commission, as well as to marginally take control of the risks of war. It is highly likely that he had been frustrated by not previously qualifying for a Commission, because he did not have the requisite paper qualifications. The War had stopped his further education, which he had worked hard at, and put paid to his progression that way. On the other hand, it had also re-opened the door for his promotion. Tom served in B.D. for two years before he was chosen for posting to an entirely different unit.

It is tempting to think that the difference between an exploded bomb and a UXB is blindingly obvious but, having seeing that Army Kinematograph Service film, it becomes apparent that these two occurrences can produce similar, but subtly different, damage effects. The UXB film's message was not to jump to a conclusion. During my research, I discovered that 'UXB' had been released on DVD, via the Imperial War Museum. It is also freely viewable on Youtube. A synopsis of the UXB film is at Chapter 14.

ITV produced a series of programmes, in 1979, entitled 'Danger UXB', starring Anthony Andrews. This 14 part drama dealt with the various developments in WW2 B.D.

technology, interwoven with some 'human interest' stories. By all accounts, the actual bomb disposal techniques and B.D. tools shown in these programmes are close to reality. The TV episodes were based on the writings of Major A. B. Hartley RE, who was himself a B.D. officer during and after WW2.They clearly demonstrate the bravery of those men and officers involved. The problem of UXBs was further complicated when Royal Engineer bomb disposal personnel began to encounter bombs fitted with anti-handling devices e.g. the Luftwaffe's ZUS40 anti-removal bomb fuze of 1940. Bomb fuzes incorporating anti-handling devices were specifically designed to kill bomb disposal personnel.

The typical German conventional high explosive (H.E.) bomb fuzes in use were :-

• type 17 fuzes – they had a delay mechanism that could be timed to operate between 3 minutes & 72 hours after deployment.

• type 50/Y fuzes – these were very sensitive anti-disturbance devices, designed to kill bomb disposal teams.

• ZUS 40 fuzes this type were designed to prevent the withdrawal of other fuzes.

• type 70 - also an anti-handing fuze, fitted to the small SD2 (butterfly) anti-personnel bombs.

There were also booby trap acoustic & magnetic sensors, a timer and a light sensitive cell usually fitted to sea mines (although sea mines were usually dealt with by Naval B.D. teams).

The BD sections were overwhelmed by the Blitz. Casualties rose and the number of unexploded bombs waiting to be dealt with increased in leaps and bounds each day. In June 1940, just 20 unexploded bombs were dealt with. This rose to 100 in July and up to 300 in August. By then over 2,000 bombs awaited their disposal. It says a lot for the officers and men involved and the speed with which they were organised in that 2,000

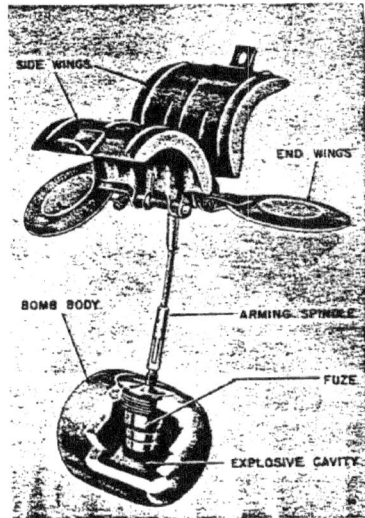

Figure 40

bombs were cleared in the first twenty days in the month of September, but by then another 3,759 had to be dealt with. In the 287 days between 21st September 1940 and 5th July 1941, 24,108 bombs were made safe and removed. Bombs were armed by connecting them to an electrical circuit in the aeroplane. When the German armourer added the fuze to the bomb, it wasn't charged and so there was no chance of an explosion whilst loading on the aircraft. Once the bomb was attached to the aircraft, an electrical socket was connected to the top of the fuze. A split second before the bomb was released from the aircraft, the fuze was instantly armed (charged) via this connection and it would detonate as it hit the target. The Germans got to know about the bomb disposal units, probably through innocent reporting in the National Press, and started to fit their fuzes with anti-tampering devices. Some had a delayed timer which was set between 5 minutes and 72 hours. Others had anti-handling devices which would detonate as soon as the fuze moved. Later during the war, they added photocell devices and as soon as it picked up a light, when it was being dealt with, whether it was sunlight or a torch, it would detonate the bomb. One of the most hazardous devices B.D. had to deal with was the *SD2 Butterfly* anti-personnel bomb. (Fig 40) They were the first 'cluster bombs' and dropped in cannisters that could contain between 8 and 108 SD2s, each one weighting 2kg. Often caught on gutters, phone wires and in trees, they would kill at 25 metres and seriously wound up to 150 metres The usual means of disposal was to detonate them on the spot, but this was not always practical to avoid undue damage and some very ingenious methods of moving them to more suitable locations for detonation were devised – often using long lengths of string and a pulley, or two. Many an SD2 landed in crop fields and proved fatal to children, farm workers and animals.

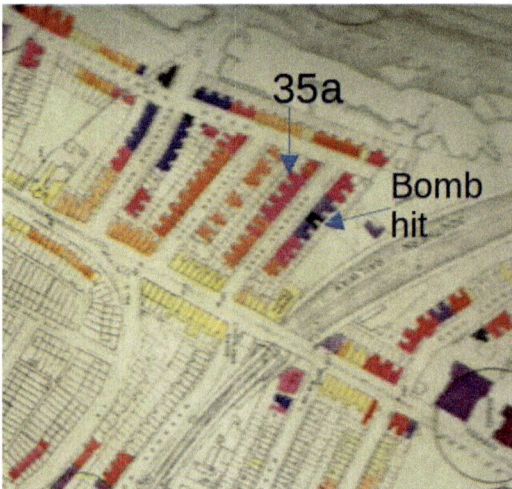

I recall my mother (Ivy) telling me that during one air raid, in 1944, a bomb had demolished a row of houses on the opposite side of the road to their flat at 35a Holdenby Road. (Fig 41)

Figure 41

At the time, my elder brother had been asleep in the front bedroom and was showered with window glass by the bomb blast. Fortunately, he had been tucked under a thick eiderdown at the time, so he was uninjured. From my time living there, in the 1960s, I remember a Mrs Peplow, who lived in a terraced house directly opposite ours at 35a. Hers was the house next door to those destroyed in that air raid. She remained a very 'nervy' disposition all those years later and would often be seen at her windows pensively looking upwards. The London County Council Bomb Map No 118 (p182) records where that Holdenby bomb struck. Properties coloured black were classed as "*destroyed*" on the maps. Being close to the conjunction of several railway lines into central London, the Crofton Park / Brockley area was often subject to air raids and latterly V1 & V2 attacks.

Our flat, at 35a, was coloured red and classed as "*damaged, but habitable*". Looking down Holdenby Road today, the difference between the original properties and the site of the bomb where they were rebuilt is clearly visible.(Fig 42). Mrs Peplow lived in the house with the black and white gable end.

Figure 42

Tom received a further promotion to Acting Captain on 1st April 1942. His tenure as C/O Bomb Disposal Stores Depot, at Long Marston, lasted from 18th December 1942 until 1st November 1943. No further detail is known about what Tom was involved in during that posting to Long Marston, but he will almost certainly have been involved with the development of equipment to tackle the UXBs problem. However, he was known to have been billeted in a house at 33, Vincent Avenue, Stratford Upon Avon (Fig 43).

Meantime, my mother (Ivy) continued to live in their rented flat in Holdenby Road.

TJG 1942
33 Vincent Avenue, Stratford Upon Avon

Figure 43

Chapter 4 - Special Operations Executive (S.O.E.)

Whatever he was doing in Bomb Disposal, Captain Tom Goodman's activity must have caught someone's eye because on 1st November 1943 the entry in his service record notes "*To be Specially Employed, retaining the rank of Captain, not remunerated from Army Funds*". This entry is a significant clue as to what was to follow. The '*not remunerated from Army funds*" phrase was used when someone was recruited to join the Special Operations Executive (S.O.E.). This was the organisation headed by

Major General Colin Gubbins who was tasked by Winston Churchill to "*set Europe ablaze*" ! S.O.E. recruited, trained and equipped both UK and foreign national agents to work behind enemy lines with the aim of disrupting and sabotaging the Axis forces. There is no formal record of how my Father was recruited, as typically, his Army

Figure 44a

record does not provide that level of detail. However, I do know that he had been to No 64, Baker Street, the headquarters of S.O.E.,several times from his casual comments on our visits up to London (Fig 44a). There are now many books on the subject of S.O.E. that describe the heroic missions that its field agents undertook. However, there are very few authoritative books that capture the technical research and 'gadget' development at establishments like Aston House and The Fyrthe. Those who joined S.O.E. did so by being invited, on

Figure 44

recommendation, and through covert approach. They usually had a special skill that S.O.E required. The photo at (Fig 44) was also in Tom's document case. By identifying the building shown behind the group in the photo, I discovered that he was a member of the 'technical / gadget section' of S.O.E. based at Aston House (Station XII) in Hertfordshire. His post designation there was "*Technical Officer*". His army form B218 describes his duties at Aston House as "*Experimental explosive devices and weapons, Inspections and Testing*", and from the photo, he was on the management team. Tom is extreme left, as viewed, in the forage cap. I also found a draft copy of Tom's *S.O.E. Personnel Record* form (AR/33) in his document case. His personal details have been completed in his own handwriting and include Next of Kin, etc. It was a draft that he must completed before later submitting a final version. It seemed to be Tom's custom to prepare a draft for important "form filling" exercises. The only S.O.E. service information that it contained was his start date of 1st November 1943.

(Fig 45 & 46)

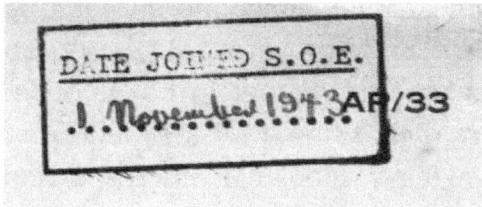

Figure 45

S.O.E. RECORD OF SERVICE

Figure 46

The National Archive files *HS8/966 and HS8/967*, at Kew, record the S.O.E. posts that Tom held at Station XII were as follows :-

HS8/966 - Page 6 - Capt T.J. GOODMAN-Devices (Station XII) - Inspection - E/Da6 - 20 Oct 43

HS 8/967 - Page 8a - Capt T.J. GOODMAN-Production (Station XII)-Inspection - E/Da5 - 21 Mar 44

Page 15 - Capt T.J. GOODMAN-Production (Station XII) - Inspection - E/Da5-29 May 44

Page 10-Capt T.J. GOODMAN - Production (Station XII) - Inspection - E/Da5- 19 Oct 44

Page 4 - Index (Personnel) Mar 45 - No longer listed.

Unfortunately, the National Archives at Kew contain very few individual personnel files for S.O.E. members. These documents were (allegedly) either destroyed in a fire at S.O.E.'s Headquarters in Baker Street after the war or they were destroyed as the organisation was wound up not long after the after the D-Day invasion proved to be so successful. To date, Tom's records appear to be amongst those destroyed. The Army records held by the M.O.D. in Glasgow do not include anything about his S.O.E. service details, because the members of that organisation "*were not in the pay of the Army*". They were paid from entirely separate funds held by S.O.E.

Originally, the 'gadget' section of S.O.E. was based at Bletchley Park (Station X), then being part of the Secret Intelligence Service (SIS), Section 'D'. Its task there was to provide special weapons and explosive devices for sabotage operations against the enemy. As their 'whiz-bang' activity increased it became clear that the reverberations they created when testing or demonstrating their devices was incompatible with the work of the radio traffic monitoring and the SIS 'Enigma' code breakers who were also stationed at Bletchley Park. So, in November 1939, that section was moved to Aston House (Station XII) in Hertfordshire. (Fig 47) This was the principal S.O.E. Station involved in the invention, testing, manufacture and supply of agents' 'gadgets' and sabotage devices. At Aston House they would also demonstrate their wares, train the trainers and sometimes demonstrate to field agents how to use the devices they were being supplied with.

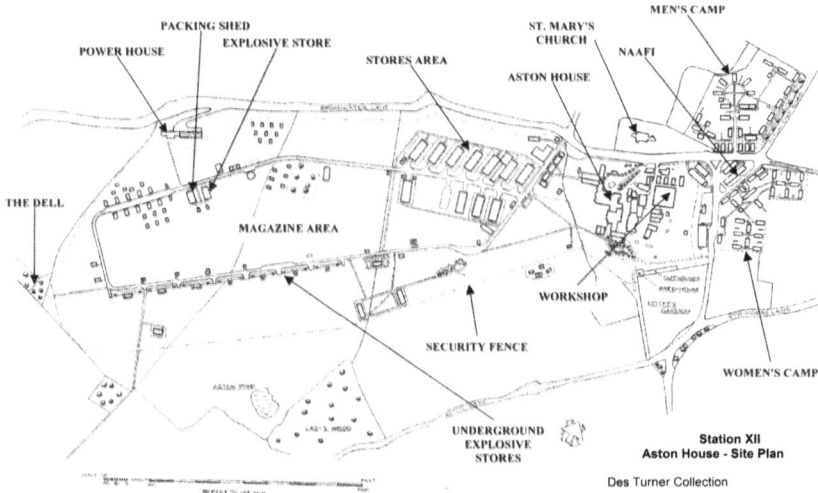

THE DELL, **POWER HOUSE**, **PACKING SHED**, **EXPLOSIVE STORE**, **STORES AREA**, **MAGAZINE AREA**, **ST. MARY'S CHURCH**, **ASTON HOUSE**, **NAAFI**, **MEN'S CAMP**, **WORKSHOP**, **SECURITY FENCE**, **UNDERGROUND EXPLOSIVE STORES**, **WOMEN'S CAMP**

Station XII
Aston House - Site Plan

Des Turner Collection

Figure 47

Later, in mid 1941, The Fyrthe (Station IX) was created a few miles away at Old Welwyn. It's purpose was to concentrate on research as Aston House became more focused on mass production. But there was still a large element of exchange between the two Stations. Both were located in large former Country Estates in the countryside not far from London. Ian Fleming, the author of 007 (James Bond) was also a member of S.O.E. and it is believed that Aston House is where his fictional character 'Q' was conceived and triggered the imaginative use of SOE type gadgetry in his 007 novels. Aston House, sometimes known as Aston Place, was built in the 17th century, with an estate of 46 acres and close to the church of St Mary. The mansion, built in Queen Anne style, was partly on 3 levels, while the wings to the east and west were lower, with the stable block on the extreme east on two floors. In the central building was an octagonal library. The mansion became the

61

officer's mess. Additional buildings were erected to meet the wartime demands, including one known as 'the factory', a NAAFI canteen, an entertainments hall in Nissen style and numerous Romney Nissen huts. The pleasure grounds (Aston Park) became the underground explosives stores and testing / demonstration grounds. It was on a visit to the site of Aston House, and the adjacent St Mary's church, that I met Church Warden, Tim Alexander. He kindly introduced me to Des Turner, who lives just a few yards down the lane from the church. Des Turner, the author, is the foremost authority on Aston House and has published four books on that specific subject. I had the privilege of meeting him in August 2022 and discovered that the same photograph that fell from my Father's document bag, when I started on this journey of discovery, was published in his first book about Aston House in 2004. That book is entitled *"Aston House, SOE, Station XII, ES6 (WD), Aston Village History Series No1"*. (Fig 48). I spent 5 months searching for a copy of

Figure 48

it and luckily found one through the powers of the internet. It was a small print run of 200, primarily intended for the villagers of Aston, many of whom had worked at Aston House during WW2 and who gave interviews and background information to Des Turner that are recorded in that book.

Colonel Leslie John Cardew Wood (Royal Engineers) was the first C.O. of Aston House and widely recognised as a James Bond 'Q' style character. He told Des Turner, in an interview, "*We invented, made, supplied and trained personnel in the use of 'toys' not only for the resistance but for all the Special Forces: Commandos, Small Boat Section, Airborne Division, and Long Range Desert Patrol. We had magazines for explosives, and sheds in which to handle them, large storehouses for incendiaries and all the rest of our' toys' and workshops wherein to experiment and manufacture. We designed and made up special explosive charges tailored for the job in hand, simple to place and fire by any Commando or Resistance worker. Many tons of explosives, as well as the devices we supplied were dropped by parachute to the Resistance to blow up bridges on D-Day. The whole essence of helping the Special Forces was speed in both invention and supply. Some may sound a little grim but I can truthfully say that we regarded the whole thing completely impersonally. The same gaiety of spirit imbued the Commandos. I met nearly all the leaders and many of their officers when they came to Aston House just before a raid for a last minute briefing or training in demolitions.*"

The group photo is on page 163 (Fig 49) of Des Turner's book. Tom (my Father) is on the extreme left hand side of the group wearing a 'forage cap'. I believe he often wore a forage cap because it could easily be tucked under his epaulette, when in the workshop or working down a hole to defuse a bomb. In fact, his document bag contained several different versions of this Aston House group photograph.

However, this one is the best composed and was obviously chosen to distribute to the members of the group. This photo is probably the last one taken of the 'management team' at Aston House, as it was taken when S.O.E. was winding down operations in March 1945. My hunch is that Tom organised the photo session and therefore selected the final one to be issued to those present in the picture, keeping the other versions himself.

Some of S.O.E.'s field operations were an unmitigated disaster, but others were a great success and contributed

Large group with Aston House in the background.
There is a member of the RAF back row extreme left. It was combined operations at E.S.6.(WD).
Ernie Welch is the only one wearing spectacles. On his left is Major Flowerdue and next to him is Mary Welch. The only other person identified is Mr. Cowdell on extreme right with hand in pocket. Probably taken at the end of the war when all were departing for a new life. Photos: By permission of Jimmy Welch.

163

Figure 49

much to winning the war. In 1942 a team of Czech and Slovak S.O.E. operatives was sent, by the Czech government-in-exile, to assassinate Reinhard Heydrich (The Butcher of Prague). They used a modified anti tank grenade of the type produced at Aston House. Following the assassination, the reprisals taken on local people, including razing to the ground the towns of Lezaky and Lidice, were terrible. Late in WW2, S.O.E. made a very significant contribution to disrupting the German response to the Allied invasion of southern Italy and then to the D-Day invasion that began in Normandy, France. In particular, the disruption that the sabotage by S.O.E.'s agents and members of the French Resistance caused to rail, road and armaments industry severely hampered the Germans' response to the Allied invasion of Normandy. Its gadgets were first used against Nazi Germany / the Italians and then Imperial Japanese Army in the South West Pacific Area.

When I met Des Turner, in August 2022, he was keen to hear about my Father's army experience to see if we could work out why he had been recruited into S.O.E. Once Des learnt that my Father had been involved in pre-war Bomb design at Woolwich Arsenal, Bomb Disposal in the early war years and that his transfer into S.O.E. happened in 1943, he concluded that this was probably in connection with the production of a sabotage fuse for destroying the German V1 flying bomb. It transpired that Bomb Disposal officers had

Figure 50

taken possession of a V1's warhead fuze from an unexploded example obtained in early 1943. The warhead the V1 carried was a 1 ton high explosive charge that caused significant damage on impact. (Fig 50)

Des Turners' historically important collection of documents, and his post war interviews with those that worked at Aston House, revealed that S.O.E. produced an identical version of the V1's warhead fuze to sabotage the flying bombs. The idea then was to deliver the sabotage fuzes to the French resistance movement who would then smuggle them into the launch assembly plants for insertion in the V1's warheads. They were designed to look identical to the original article, but would detonate the V1s prematurely, either as they were being launched up their launch ramp, or at some point afterwards during its flight. V1s were given their pre-flight final assembly, including arming of the warhead, in special buildings erected at each launch site along the French coast. Prior to launch, the Fuze was fitted to the warhead and once on the launch ramp a lanyard was attached to a 'pull pin' in the Fuze. When the V1 was launched up the ramp, the lanyard pulled out the pin and the fuze would be armed in the warhead. It is thought these sabotage fuzes had variable time delay in order to try and disguise the reason for the vehicles failure, by prematurely exploding, after they had left the ramp. There are several launch failures to be seen in the V1 launch site, located in The Pas de Calais, annotated B,C,D & E in this RAF reconnaissance photo. (Fig 51). It was taken after a British bombing raid to destroy the site of a V1 assembly building and launch ramp installation.

Figure 51

Given Tom's background and the timing of his transfer into S.O.E. it does seem highly probable they wanted Captain Goodman's engineering, bomb design and Bomb Disposal experience for the V1 sabotage fuze project. (Fig 52)

The German Army's field records show that, from June 1944, about 8,000 V1s were launched towards England. Interestingly, there were many reported instances of an unexplained explosion as the V1s took off. Des Turner's book indicates that about 1,000 of the V1s exploded on take off. It isn't known how many such launch failures were actually due to sabotage, but a good proportion must have been down to the work of S.O.E. It should not be forgotten that the Germans began to record the names of the slave workers that assembled each V1 and V2. They took heavy reprisals if the weapons they had worked on failed to perform correctly. Hence the sabotage fuze's delayed action to try and disguise the fact that it had been sabotaged. It is probable that the sabotage fuze also included a variable delay to further disguise the cause of the premature detonations.

The German 80s Fuse and Gaine

PRO HS 7/16

The V-1 (Vergeltung-1 - Retaliation) was a pilot-less aircraft that travelled at a speed of 400 miles per hour at a height of 3,000 feet and had a range of about 130 miles. We British called them Doodle-Bugs or Buzz Bombs to nullify the unprecedented fear of this terror weapon. About 8,000 V-1 bombs were launched, 1000 crashed immediately after take off. Civilian casualties amounted to 6,184 with 17,981 injured. The last V-1 came down at Datchworth, Herts.

Figure 52

In the early 1960s Tom, expressed great interest in seeing the Imperial War Museum's new display where, amongst other items, a V1 was being exhibited. I went with him to this exhibition and recall that he took a very close interest in the V1 that was displayed, although at the time he did not say what his interest was, I now believe I know why he wanted to see it. (Fig 53)

Figure 53

One day, around the same time, (I was about 12yrs old) we were walking along the pavement in Holdenby Road when I spied a dog's 'poo' on the kerb stone. I was about to nudge it into the gutter, with my foot, when Tom held me back, smiled, and said *"no, don't do that - it might go bang* !". I remember looking at him quizzically and didn't understand what was behind his comment - until many years later. At Aston House he had, of course, been involved in producing all sorts of field agent's booby trap devices, including plastic explosive disguised as dog, horse and camel poo and even rats stuffed with it. The rats were deposited in coal heaps, by the resistance, to blow up the German munitions factory boiler installations and also in their steam locomotive coal tenders for the same effect.

Another item that S.O.E. produced and supplied to troops of the airborne divisions was a fold up motor bike that could be put in a container and dropped by parachute to onto foreign soil. This was the *Welbike.* Having watched a war film on TV with my Father one day, when a *Welbike* was shown in use, I recall him saying that, during the war, he had once 'borrowed' a fold up motor bike to travel home to see my mother. On the way there and back he had been stopped several times because rumours were circulating that German parachutists had been dropped in the countryside with motor bikes just like these. Luckily, he was in uniform and had his full Military ID with him. I understand that he didn't try doing that journey again because it was a bit too risky to be mistaken for a German parachutist and he said the *Welbike* was quite an uncomfortable ride for long journeys. (Fig 54)

In the course of my research, I found another book reference with an interesting and direct connection to Tom. It was published by The Imperial War

Figure 54

Museum (IWM), entitled *The British Spy Manual*. It's a reproduction of the Top Secret *"Descriptive Catalogue of Special Devices and Supplies Vol 2"* that Aston House (M.O.I. S.P.) produced in 1944/5 for agents to select items from, to take with them on their missions.

When Tom died, I was given several of his woodworking hand tools. Leafing through the IWM's reproduction catalogue I spotted some of those (Tom's) hand tools in the catalogue (Vol 2 Section F,p233), (Fig 55)

Figure 55

Each of those I had inherited, were identical to the items catalogued, except they had not been *"hollowed out for the concealment of documents or money"*. (Fig 56).

Figure 56

Those
tools are as follows :-

-Two wood planes and a mallet (p 233).

- Catalogue No G 71,a 'screwdriver, plain, small' (p60)

- Catalogue No G 73 & G73a 'Pliers, Insulated & Plain (p57)

- Catalogue No J 137, 'Knives, Dagger Jack, single blade (p56). It had a locking mechanism to prevent the blade from closing on the users hand.

Tom's example of the Knife (Cat. No J137) was kept in his tool box, when we lived in Chiswick, but it has become lost over time. Of interest is the fact that his knife had the tip of the blade snapped off. I came across it when rummaging in his tool box and asked him how the blade had been broken off. He just replied *"I stuck it in and twisted it"* Quite what

71

that meant, I did not like to ask at the time. I presume that, as Tom was still at Aston House during it's winding down phase, these catalogue items were no longer required for operational purposes. They would probably have been disposed of and so I assume he brought them home to put them into practical use.

Aston House and its grounds (Fig 57) were situated near Hemel Hampstead, in Hertfordshire. After the War it was handed back to the civil authorities. However, the work that went on there during WW2 had taken a very heavy toll on the building's fabric. So, after a brief spell as offices for Stevenage Town Council, it was demolished in 1961. Private houses and a

ASTON HOUSE *Herts. (Demolished)*
R&D, Production of Sabotage Weapons

Figure 57

Golf Course have since been built in the grounds. All that remains now is the original Coach House, which has been converted into smart private accommodation.

Across from the original entrance drive to Aston House, now renamed Yeoman's Drive in memory of the last private owner in 1939, is the parish Church of St Mary's. The staff of Aston House used to attend it. (Fig 58)

To the rear of the church, just inside the door, there is a brass plaque acknowledging that *"The chiming apparatus*

(of the church clock) was the gift of the Military and Civilian Personnel of Experimental Station 6 (WD), Aston House, in 1945" (Fig.59).

Experimental Station 6(WD) is yet another of the names given to Station XII by its C/O, Colonel Leslie John Cardew-Wood R.E., in an attempt to conceal its real purpose from the populace at large, although many locals did indeed work there and remained living in Aston village after Aston House's SOE activities were wound down in late 1945.

Figure 58

Figure 59

73

Chapter 5 - Services Reconnaissance Department

(Also known as Z Force, Force 137 and Special Operations Australia)

The continuing success of the Allied invasion of France, which started on D-Day the 6th June 1944, meant that by late 1945 S.O.E.'s relevance in Europe was greatly reduced. There was also a very heavy cost involved in maintaining S.O.E.'s operations. So, it was decided to wind the organisation down rapidly. In a letter dated 2nd November 1944, from Maurice Lubbock, Ministry of Information, Special Projects.(M.O.I. S.P.), the forerunner of today's MI6, Tom was told he could not be retained at Aston House after 30th November 1944 and that he would soon be receiving further instructions about his next posting.

Although Tom was supposed to be re-deployed at the end of November 1944, the next posting listed in his service history appears as :- *"Authority = M.O.I.(S.P.), 24th March 1945 - Proceeded Overseas by Air- to be G.S.O. III (VII I/812/2), also "without pay and allowances from Army funds"*. Another covert organisation posting. This posting was under the heading of *"The Ministry of Information, Special Projects, General Staff Officer III. M.O.I.(SP)"*.

On 19th March 1945 he was issued with Passport No 60753, by The Foreign Office. Tom's record does not indicate his destination on that journey. However, through the power of the internet, I unearthed an immigration certificate in the *"Baltimore Immigration Passenger Lists"* which shows that Tom arrived in the United States on 27th March 1945. He was listed on that flight document as a *"Civilian"* and his address in America was given as "*c/o British Security Coordination*". (Fig 60)

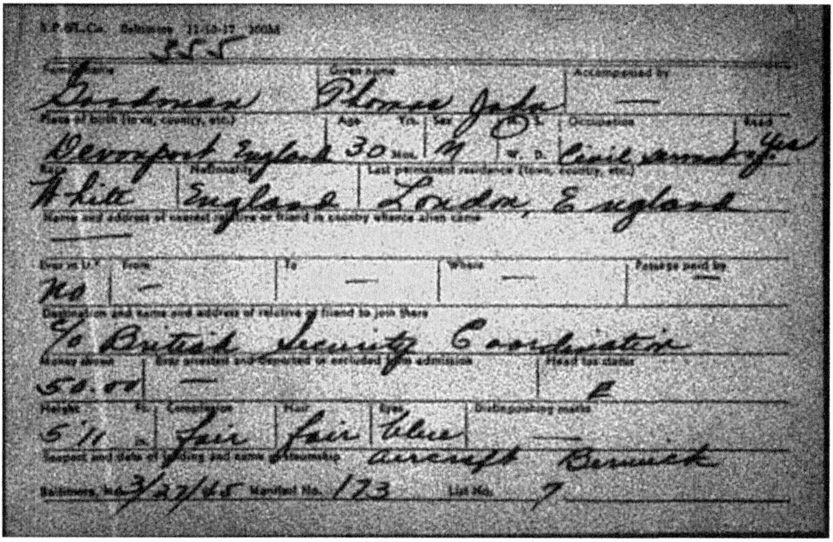
355
Given name / Accompanied by
Place of birth (town, country, etc.) — Devonport England — Age 30 Yrs. — Sex M — Occupation: Civil servant — Read: Yes
Race: White — Nationality: England — Last permanent residence (town, country, etc.): London, England
Name and address of nearest relative or friend in country whence alien came: —
Ever in U.S.: No — From: — — To: — — Where: — — Passage paid by: —
Destination and name and address of relative or friend to join there: c/o British Security Coordination
Money shown: 50.00 — Ever arrested and deported or excluded from admission: — — Head tax status
Height: 5 ft. 11 in. — Complexion: fair — Hair: fair — Eyes: blue — Distinguishing marks: —
Seaport and date of landing and name of steamship: Aircraft Berwick
Baltimore, Md. 3/27/45 Manifest No. 173 List No. 7

Figure 60

British Security Coordination (B.S.C.) was the cover name given to the secret organisation sanctioned by Winston Churchill and with the support of both President Franklin D. Roosevelt and the chief of the US Office of Strategic Services (OSS). Early in WW2 there were real difficulties with formal US co-operation with the British war effort, because of the USA's Neutrality Acts of the 1930s that, theoretically, prevented America lending support to either side in the War. That is, before the Japanese Bombing of Pearl Harbour in December 1941, when the United States joined the Allied cause head on.

B.S.C. was set up in May 1940 by the British Secret Intelligence Service (SIS). It was for intelligence gathering and propaganda services to counter German activity and prevent sabotage against British interests in America and also to bolster pro-British opinion in the Americas. It operated under the cover of The British Passport Office from the 35th and 36th floors of The Rockefeller Centre, New York. From there it influenced the news coverage of several important newspapers, including the New York Post, Herald Tribune and The Baltimore Sun. The anti-German stories emanating from its offices, via these publications, would be picked up by other news organisations and media outlets which helped to turn public opinion in favour of the British cause. It also had an important centre for radio communications between the USA and the UK using a powerful radio transceiver, code named *HYDRA*. This was located at *Camp-X*, just over the Canadian border in Whitby, on the shores of Lake Ontario. *Camp-X* was also known as STS 103 (Special Training School) an adjunct of SOE's UK training structure for field agents who were of US and Canadian origin. They were drilled in the methods of "secret warfare" and destined to be dropped into occupied Europe to operate "in the field". Interestingly, the author Ian Fleming was also a member of BSC, around about this time.

The US immigration list (Fig 60) shows that Tom landed at Baltimore on "*Aircraft – Berwick*", a BOAC Boeing B314A 'Clipper' flying boat. BOAC operated 3 aircraft of this type.

No.1 was G-AGBZ '*Bristol*',

No.2 was G-AGCA '*Berwick*' (Fig 61) and

No.3. was G-AGCB '*Bangor*'.

Figure 61

They were referred to by these idents for all their operational movements.

The photo (Fig 62) is of the Pan American terminus at Baltimore which they shared with the BOAC Clipper aircraft. All the heavy maintenance for BOAC's Boeing B314s was completed there as well.

Figure 62

The *Poole Flying Boats Celebration* have confirmed, from their flight records of the time, that Berwick left Baltimore,

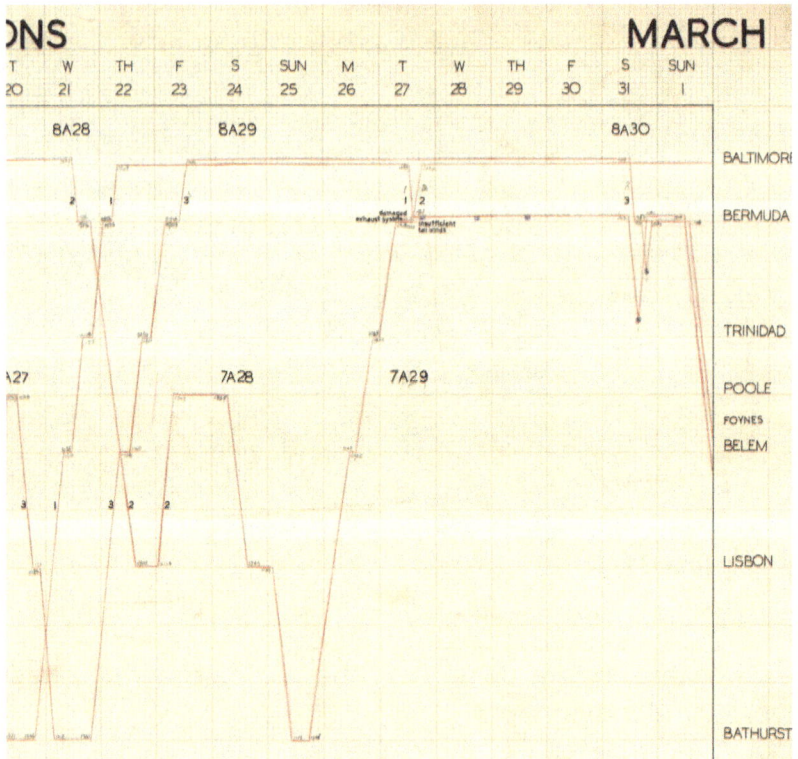

Figure 63

bound for Pool as flight 8A28 on 21 March 1945 flying via Bermuda and Lisbon, arriving at Poole on 23 Mar 45. When Tom boarded *Berwick* at Poole Harbour, the flight number became 7A28. (Fig 63) *Berwick* departed from Poole on 24 Mar at 8.38am and proceeded to Lisbon (Portugal), arriving at 2.09pm the same day. It stayed in Lisbon until 4.43am the next morning when it departed, bound for Bathurst (now known as Banjul) in The Gambia), arriving at 12.59pm on 25 March. At 5.05pm on 25 March 1945 *Berwick* departed Bathurst bound for Belem (a large city in northern Brazil

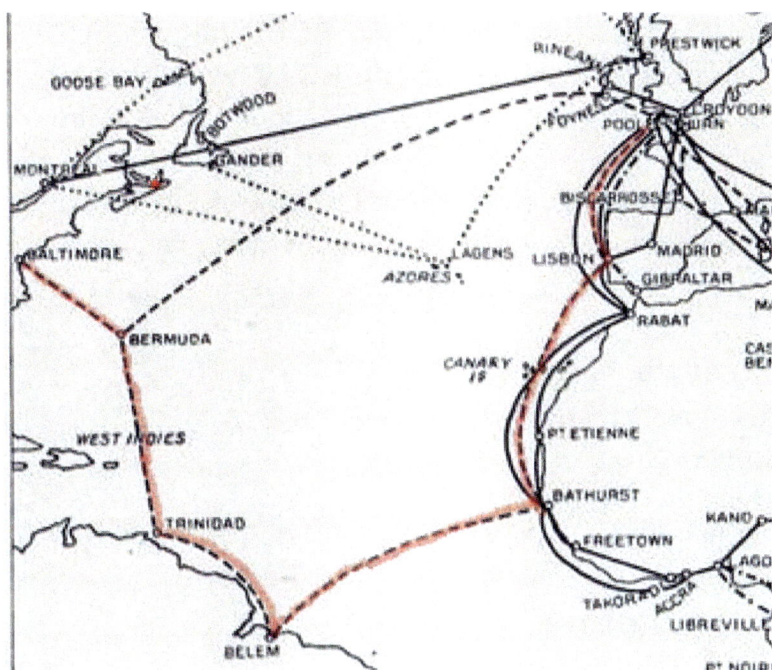

Figure 64

close to the mouth of the Amazon) where it arrived on the 26 March at 9.00am. Departure from Belem, bound for Trinidad, was at 11.05am the same morning. *Berwick* arrived in Trinidad at 6.22pm the same day (26th March). It departed for Bermuda at 9.35pm and arrived there at 08.28am on the morning of 27 March. Berwick's flight was delayed in Bermuda while a damaged exhaust system on one of the engines was fixed. It then left Bermuda at 1.54pm and arrived at The Pan Am Terminus, Baltimore, on 27th March at 7.34pm. A journey of around 8,800 miles that was completed in 4 days. (Fig 64)

Originally, *Berwick* was purchased by Pan American Airways but they immediately sold her to BOAC (reg. G-AGCA) in 1941 to help with the war effort. BOAC was formed by an Act of Parliament in November 1939 to nationalise the UK's airlines into one organisation, as an aid to the War effort. BOAC had their flying boat landing facility in the USA at Baltimore (Harbor Field) and that was its main U.S. Operating Base during the war for its "flying boat" service, which ran four times a week to Baltimore from Poole Harbour, in Dorset (Fig 65), until the service was ended in 1948, when Berwick was sold off.

Figure 65

There was also a 'great circle' northern route from the UK to the USA, from Poole via Foynes (Ireland) and Botwood (Newfoundland, Canada) to Baltimore (USA). However, this route was only operated during the summer months, as sea ice was a problem during the winter time. This is why Tom's flight operated via the more southerly route, which had no icing problems due to the warmer waters from the Gulf Stream entering the Atlantic.

The picture at (Fig 66) shows 'Berwick' being moored after a trans-Atlantic flight. This is the same aircraft that also carried both Winston Churchill and Lord Beaverbrook

80

(Minister of Aircraft Production) back to the United Kingdom in mid January, 1942, after Churchill's extended stay in the United States, following the Japanese bombing of Pearl Harbour. Churchill was the first head of government to make a trans-Atlantic crossing by plane. It was also the first occasion that an

Figure 66

oxygen mask was modified to enable the user to smoke a cigar. The Boeing B-314A was a true aerial ocean liner that was both efficient and elegant and in a class of its own. It could carry up to 74 passengers and 10 crew. In pre war days there was only one passenger level - First Class. The aircraft's build employed ship construction techniques with a compartmented double bottom and full-depth, forward and aft, watertight bulkheads, producing a 106-foot overall length. The massive, three-section, high-mounted wing, which spanned 152 feet, was subdivided into a centre, hull-integral section that extended beyond either side's inner engine nacelles, and two outer, watertight sections. Its centre wing spar, supported by the upper fuselage, featured both increased strength and internal volume, while its 4,200-gallon fuel capacity was distributed between wing centre section and lower-fuselage extending "sponson" tanks, giving it a maximum range of up to 5,200 miles, depending upon the payload. Appearing like mini-wings, these sponsons provided lateral, in-water stability, obviating the need for traditional wing floats, and alternatively served as passenger entry platforms leading to the cabin door. So cavernous were the main wings, that they contained interior catwalks to permit in-flight inspection and maintenance of both their structure and to monitor the state of the engines.

After Tom's arrival in the USA on 27th March, his next known location is on 10th April, 14 days later. Tempting as it is to think that Tom was "active" with BSC, it is most probable that his association with the organisation was simply a convenient cover for his transportation from the UK into America and then onward, overland, to San Diego, California where he can next be traced.

Figure 67

Today, the Amtrak journey from Baltimore to San Diego takes 79 hours (Fig 67). That service runs just once a day. It is a journey of 2,292 miles in about 79 hours. The lowest ticket today costs £305. Tom was noted as carrying £50 in cash on his arrival in Baltimore (Fig 60). In today's values (2024) that £50 equates to approximately £2,600, so he had plenty of funding for the journey cross continental America. Amongst the papers in Tom's document case were two telegrams. Both brought news regarding the welfare of his second son, Peter. The first gave news of Peter's birth on the 7th April 1945 and that Peter's condition was "*serious*". The second telegram brought the news that Peter had died on 8th April 1945, but "*Mother normal*". (Fig 68)

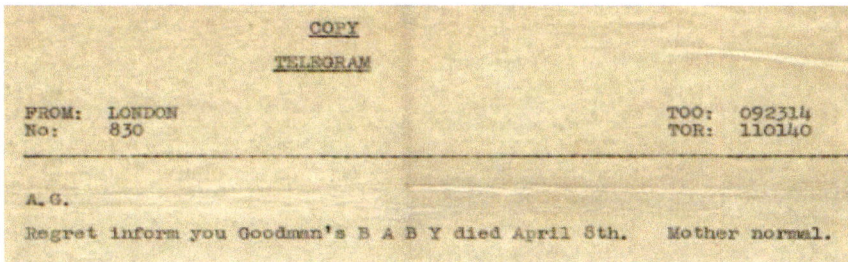

Figure 68

Quite where Tom was on the 7th and 8th April, and how soon after that event he was given the bad news, is presently unknown. The London station that originated those telegrams (*London)* and where they were received is also an unknown. (TOO = Time of Origination, TOR = time of receipt). My mother (Ivy) was in Lewisham Hospital for Peter's birth. She never mentioned the circumstances of his death. I suspect she took the loss with great fortitude as, although the War in Europe had almost come to an end, the war with the Japanese was still raging on and many civilians in England were still suffering great hardship and personal loss, together with mental and physical suffering.

Tom's departure from the USA was on an RAF flight, on 10th April 1945. He left from San Diego, aboard aircraft JT981 bound for Hickam Field, Honolulu. (Fig 69). It was an RAF "*Pacific Airways*" flight, piloted by Squadron Leader Richard D.F.C. This Clearance Declaration document was unearthed by David Armstrong of the Special Operations Executive interest group.

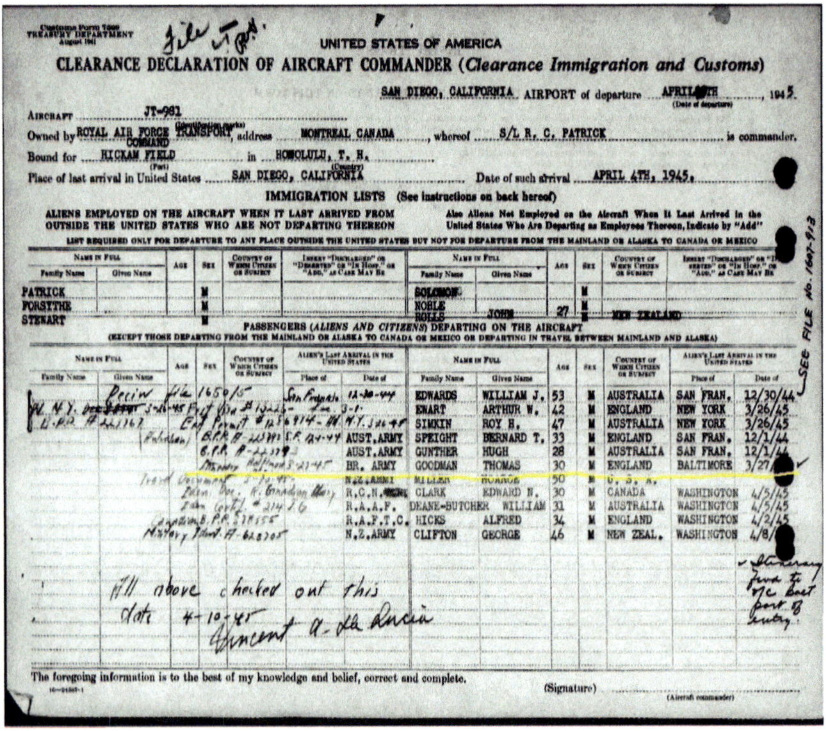

Customs Form 7509
TREASURY DEPARTMENT
August 1941

UNITED STATES OF AMERICA

CLEARANCE DECLARATION OF AIRCRAFT COMMANDER (*Clearance Immigration and Customs*)

SAN DIEGO, CALIFORNIA AIRPORT of departure APRIL ... TH, 1945 (Date of departure)

Aircraft JT-981 (Identification marks)

Owned by ROYAL AIR FORCE TRANSPORT COMMAND, address MONTREAL CANADA, whereof S/L R. C. PATRICK is commander.

Bound for HICKAM FIELD (Port) in HONOLULU, T. H. (Country)

Place of last arrival in United States SAN DIEGO, CALIFORNIA Date of such arrival APRIL 4TH, 1945.

IMMIGRATION LISTS (See instructions on back hereof)

ALIENS EMPLOYED ON THE AIRCRAFT WHEN IT LAST ARRIVED FROM OUTSIDE THE UNITED STATES WHO ARE NOT DEPARTING THEREON

Also Aliens Not Employed on the Aircraft When It Last Arrived in the United States Who Are Departing as Employees Thereon, Indicate by "Add"

LIST REQUIRED ONLY FOR DEPARTURE TO ANY PLACE OUTSIDE THE UNITED STATES BUT NOT FOR DEPARTURE FROM THE MAINLAND OR ALASKA TO CANADA OR MEXICO

Family Name	Given Name	Age	Sex	Country of Which Citizen or Subject	Insert "Discharged" or "Deserted" or "In Hosp." or "Add," as Case May Be	Family Name	Given Name	Age	Sex	Country of Which Citizen or Subject	Insert "Discharged" or "Deserted" or "In Hosp." or "Add," as Case May Be
PATRICK			M			SOLOMON			M		
FORSYTHE			M			NOBLE			M		
STEWART			M			ROLLS	JOHN	27	M	NEW ZEALAND	

PASSENGERS (*ALIENS AND CITIZENS*) DEPARTING ON THE AIRCRAFT
(EXCEPT THOSE DEPARTING FROM THE MAINLAND OR ALASKA TO CANADA OR MEXICO OR DEPARTING IN TRAVEL BETWEEN MAINLAND AND ALASKA)

	Family Name	Given Name	Age	Sex	Country of Which Citizen or Subject	Alien's Last Arrival in the United States: Place of	Date of
	EDWARDS	WILLIAM J.	53	M	AUSTRALIA	SAN FRAN.	12/30/44
	EWART	ARTHUR W.	42	M	ENGLAND	NEW YORK	3/26/45
	SIMKIN	ROY H.	47	M	AUSTRALIA	NEW YORK	3/26/45
AUST.ARMY	SPEIGHT	BERNARD T.	33	M	ENGLAND	SAN FRAN.	12/1/44
AUST.ARMY	GUNTHER	HUGH	28	M	AUSTRALIA	SAN FRAN.	12/1/4
BR. ARMY	GOODMAN	THOMAS	30	M	ENGLAND	BALTIMORE	3/27/
N.Z.ARMY	MILLER	HORACE	50	M	U. S. A.		
R.C.N.	CLARK	EDWARD N.	30	M	CANADA	WASHINGTON	4/5/45
R.A.A.F.	DEANE-BUTCHER	WILLIAM	31	M	AUSTRALIA	WASHINGTON	4/5/45
R.A.F.T.C.	HICKS	ALFRED	34	M	ENGLAND	WASHINGTON	4/2/45
N.Z.ARMY	CLIFTON	GEORGE	46	M	NEW ZEAL.	WASHINGTON	4/8/

All above checked out this date 4-10-45

SEE FILE No. 1607-913

The foregoing information is to the best of my knowledge and belief, correct and complete.

(Signature) .... (Aircraft commander)

Figure 69

Aircraft JT891 was a Liberator C.IX of 231 Squadron RAF, a passenger transport development of the US Navy Privateer

Figure 70

aircraft, itself a development of the earlier B24 Liberator bomber, which was then lengthened to become the C87. (Fig 70)

The Privateer was converted into a Liberator C.IX by lengthening the fuselage by 7 feet and rotating the engine cowlings by 90 degrees so the air intakes were above and below the engine, instead of on the sides. In addition to these exterior modifications, the armaments were removed, windows were added to the fuselage and seating replaced the bomb bay and waist gunner compartments.

A large loading door was cut into the side of the rear fuselage and fairings were installed where the nose and tail gun turrets had been. A crew of four and 28 passengers could be carried or 16,641 pounds of cargo in the all-freight configuration. A hinged nose allowed up to 1600 pounds of cargo to be carried in the forward section. All surviving RAF Liberator C.IXs, except one, were *'struck off charge'* in April 1946 and either returned to the US Navy or else were scrapped. Only 39 of the C.IX version were built.

Figure 71

The C.IX was supposedly of a similar gross unloaded weight to the Privateer, but a lesser supercharger had been used in the engines and so performance was negatively impacted. Fully loaded, the C.IX would have had a lower range and top speed than the bomber variants due to its lower altitude ceiling and worse supercharger capabilities. The range of the Liberator C.IX could be up to 3,500 miles with a top speed of approximately 200 mph, subject to the payload and flight altitude. The total distance of that journey was approximately 8,457 miles.(Fig 71) There would have been stop overs for refuelling and crew rest, rather than the non-stop travel to Australia that we know today. Equally amazing is the fact that navigation was either by the stars - or just dead reckoning.

San Diego (Hamilton Field) to Hickam Field, Honolulu (Pearl Harbour) is 2,416 miles so it is likely that that leg took around 12 hours. Hickam Field to Canton Island is 1,904 miles, Canton Island to Fiji is 1,255 miles, Fiji to Auckland is 1,327 miles and Auckland to Sydney is 1,355 miles.

On the flight with Tom was Brigadier George Clifton D.S.O., of the New Zealand Army. He was on a repatriation flight back to New Zealand, having escaped from the German P.O.W. Camp Oflag XII B on 22nd March 1945. He escaped taking advantage of an Allied air attack that damaged the camp's perimeter fencing. Although his escape route lay through a forbidden zone, he walked for four days and three nights until he was just behind the German lines near Weis. He hid until the enemy retreated during the night and then reported to an American unit the next morning. Brigadier Clifton had attempted escape on a number of occasions and was wounded during one of them. He was classed as "recidivist escapee". He had initially been captured in 1942 near El Alamein and was interrogated by Field Marshal Rommel. After his return, Brigadier Clifton went on to serve with 'Jayforce' at the 2nd New Zealand Expeditionary Force's Headquarters, in Japan

The RAF's experience with the Liberator (Consolidated) C.IX was not a happy one. Three were lost in fatal crashes. There was speculation that something was wrong with the structural integrity of the aircraft after the "passenger conversions" had taken place.

The Pilot of JT981, on Tom's passage, was Squadron Leader Richard Patrick DFC. After receiving his wings, Richard Patrick joined No. 206 Squadron. It was a Coastal Command unit initially operating Ansons, and later Hudsons, on the outbreak of hostilities in September 1939. He participated in over 80 sorties in the period leading up to December 1940, and another dozen or so from March to September 1941. The sorties mainly comprised reconnaissance work, convoy patrols and anti-submarine operations, the latter including an attack on a U-Boat off Lundy Island on 20 September 1939. Patrick also attacked three E-Boats with machine-gun fire in April 1941, Returning to No. 206 Squadron for a second tour of operations in the following year, as Acting Squadron Leader and latterly piloting Fortress aircraft. He participated in at least four anti-U-boat strikes, one of them on 9 February 1943, bearing all the hallmarks of a successful kill: *'Attacked U-Boat, direct hit. U-Boat lifted bodily, slewed 30 degrees. U-Boat sank straight down and an up-rush of bubbles was seen'.* In another attack with six depth-charges on 24 April, a U-Boat was seen to crash-dive and left a slight scum on the surface afterwards. Patrick, who also piloted one of No 12 Squadron's Hudsons in the Thousand Bomber Raid on Bremen in late June 1942, was finally rested in February 1944, returning to the U.K. from 206's latest base at Lagens, in the Azores. Subsequently, Patrick held a regular commission after the War's end. After his retirement Patrick went on to found a company involved in the supply of aircraft engineering components.

Tom's Australian Service book records the date of his enlistment in their Army as 10th July 1945, with service No VB173594 (S.O.A. No AKX137). (Fig 72)

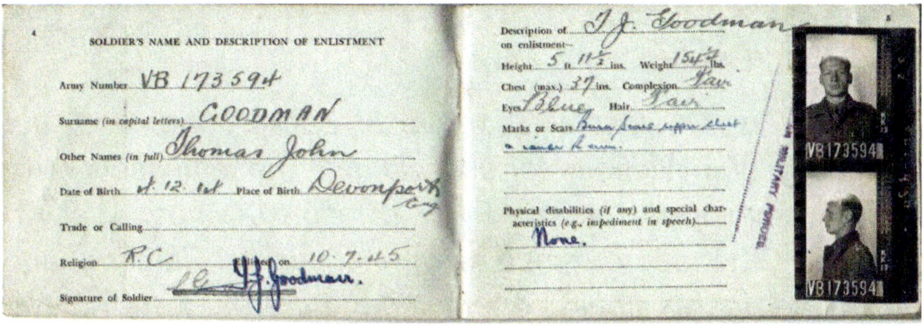
SOLDIER'S NAME AND DESCRIPTION OF ENLISTMENT

Army Number VB 173594

Surname (in capital letters) GOODMAN

Other Names (in full) Thomas John

Date of Birth ... Place of Birth Devonport

Trade or Calling

Religion R.C ... on 10.7.45

Signature of Soldier T.J. Goodman

Description of T.J. Goodman on enlistment—

Height 5 ft 11½ ins. Weight 154½ lbs.

Chest (max.) 37 ins. Complexion Fair

Eyes Blue Hair Fair

Marks or Scars

Physical disabilities (if any) and special characteristics (e.g., impediment in speech) None.

VB173594

VB173594

Figure 72

However, that is about 16 weeks after he left San Diego on 10th March 1945. His travelling companion on that flight was Brigadier Clifton, who is reported in his local press to have arrived back in New Zealand in early April 1945. So what was Tom doing meantime ?

Through Fred Judge, another member of the Special Operations Executive interest group, I discovered that Tom's first assignment in Australia is believed to have been as a Welfreighter Instructor on Garden Island, a secret training base, just offshore from Freemantle near Perth in Western Australia. Around the same time this fact emerged, The National Archive Australia unearthed Tom's Personnel record card. It details Tom's "*Sworn in Date*" as 16th April

1945. That is just 6 days after leaving San Diego. His "*Sworn Out*" date is recorded as 22 October 1945. (Fig 73).

```
GOODMAN, T.J.,
  VB 173594,  Capt.                      AKX 137

Sworn-in 16.4.45.
(ex 12,9 & 15 - to work as Stores).
  SwornOut 22.10.45.
```

Figure 73

Fred Judge wrote :-

"Picked up on Capt. Goodman's background and the possibility of a Welfreighter association. These vessels were S.O.E. developed (at The Fyrth (Station IX) near Welwyn Garden City) as four-man submersibles for landing and supplying agents behind enemy lines but they were not too successful."

Late in 1944 to possibly mid-1945 some were shipped to Fremantle Western Australia as part of SRD (Z Unit). Of around 150 built in the U.K. between 8 and 12 of the vessels were landed and members of the Services Reconnaissance Department [SRD] Special Ops teams trained on them at Garden island south of Perth, WA - the present site of HMAS Stirling, the RAN's West Coast headquarters base.

Extensive trials conducted ie towing trials and exercises using high-powered motor launches and Motor Torpedo Boats. They were based out of Garden Island for Z Special Unit Officers training at nearby Careening Camp. Welfreighters were also used in Hong Kong to ferry repatriated ex-POWs (amongst other things) out to hospital vessels.

The Welfreighters were primarily designed to carry cylinders of supplies on their foredeck that could be floated ashore to

Figure 74

commandos at pre-arranged supply points on an enemy coast. With a range of 600 nautical miles and a speed of eight knots, in Australia they were intended for use in conjunction with the 'Snake Class' Special Ops lugger-style craft, specially designed and built in Fremantle and Melbourne during WWII to look like native fishing vessels. Not much more is publicly known about their use as, by their very nature, these operations were kept entirely secret." (Fig 74) So, this would appear to account for the joining date (TOS) gap between 16th April and 10th July 1945 in his service book.

After his stint as a Welfreighter instructor, Tom was destined for Melbourne, in the State of Victoria, Australia. There he was attached to the Australian Army's equivalent of S.O.E H.Q. Today it is known as "Z Special Unit". At the time it had several cover names i.e. the Inter-Allied Services Department (I.S.D.), Services Reconnaissance Department (S.R.D), Special Operations Australia (S.O.A) and latterly Z Force. Through my research, I discovered a series of five volumes entitled *"The Official History of Special Operations, Australia"*. The material for these volumes was replicated directly from the original S.O.A. records held in the National Archives of Australia (N.A.A.). Once in Melbourne, Tom joined the Rear HQ Staff of S.R.D. On page 192 of *The Official History of Special Operations, Australia, Volume 1.* Tom is shown on a *SECRET* Organisation chart dated *"31st July 1945"*.

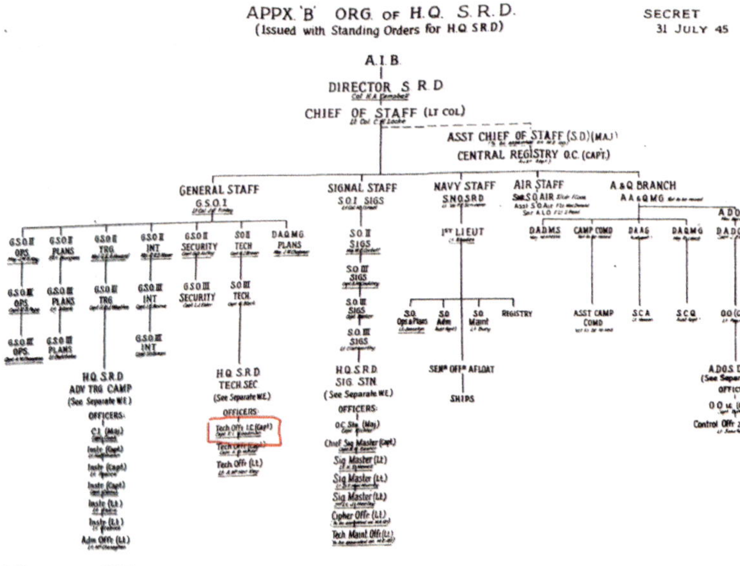

Figure 75

His post is on the General Staff and shown as *"Technical Officer, In Charge (Capt)"*- highlighted in red on (Fig 75)

Tom is also listed on another H.Q. S.R.D. family tree in the N.A.A. archive.(Fig 76)

His Z Force record, in Fred Judge's S.O.E. Staff cardex, is *"Australian Army No VB173594, SOA No AKX137, RE, Tech Officer, production & inspection, STA XII, Aston House, ME 100, Z Special Unit, SRD, Welfreighter instructor at Freemantle. Operation ETHELRED (surrender of Hong Kong)."*

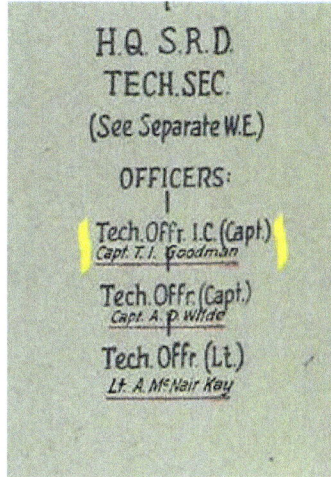

Figure 76

It was a similar role to the one he held in S.O.E. and Tom was obviously there to provide the Australian Special Operations (SRD) with the knowledge he gained at Aston House (Station XII) in the continuing fight against the Japanese. Many of the 'gadgets' invented by S.O.E. at Aston House and The Fyrth, for use in Europe, were shared with and replicated by the Australians and adapted for use in the South West Pacific Theatre conditions. This included the Welfreighter, Welcanoe, Welbike, the Sten gun, pencil fuzes, plastic explosive booby traps and many more intriguing items from the *British Spy Manual Catalogue* ! S.R.D. conducted field operations into the Japanese held areas North of Australia. Like S.O.E's, some of these operations were stunning successes while others were tragic failures. Throughout the War in the Pacific, the specially selected operatives of S.R.D (Force Z) proved

93

themselves many times over on operations' in the jungles and on the beaches of modern day Papua New Guinea, Timor Leste, Malaysia, Vietnam and Indonesia.

The "Z" men, as they are known today, were the best of the Australian best, an elite force, prepared by some of the toughest training available and backed up by the best technology of the day. Tom's name is also listed in the National Archives of Australia (Document ref A3269 / H17). It records the *"SRD's Officers and Senior NCOs believed to have survived the War"* It also indicates Tom's service "spot dates" (*4:45 to 8:45*) and the last WW2 Operation, during the hostilities, that he took part in.(Fig 77).

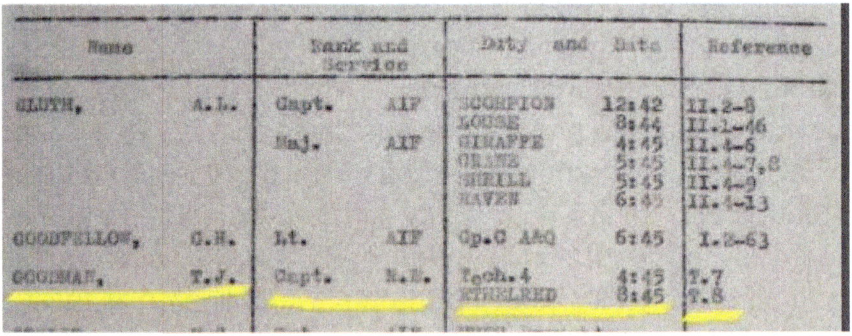

Name		Rank and Service		Duty and Date		Reference
GLUTH,	A.L.	Capt.	AIF	SCORPION	12:42	II.2-8
				LOUSE	8:44	II.1-46
		Maj.	AIF	GIRAFFE	4:45	II.4-6
				CRANE	5:45	II.4-7,8
				SHRILL	5:45	II.4-9
				RAVEN	6:45	II.4-13
GOODFELLOW,	G.H.	Lt.	AIF	Op.O AAQ	6:45	I.2-63
GOODMAN,	T.J.	Capt.	R.E.	Tech.4	4:45	T.7
				XTHELRED	8:45	T.8

Figure 77

94

Chapter 6 - Operation Ethelred (British Pacific Fleet)

When the first Atomic bombs were dropped on Hiroshima and Nagasaki, in August 1945, the British South Pacific Fleet was based in Sydney harbour. On 15th August 1945, Emperor Hirohito announced the Japanese Empire's surrender.

In the Australian National Archives, there is an S.R.D. Rear Headquarters, Technical Report (NAA A3269 R3/A) which records that *"on 17th August 1945,Capt. T J Goodman….. left Melbourne to take up duties with Ethelred Project"*. He wasn't alone in this departure, but accompanied by four other British Army soldiers from the same section. (Fig 78)

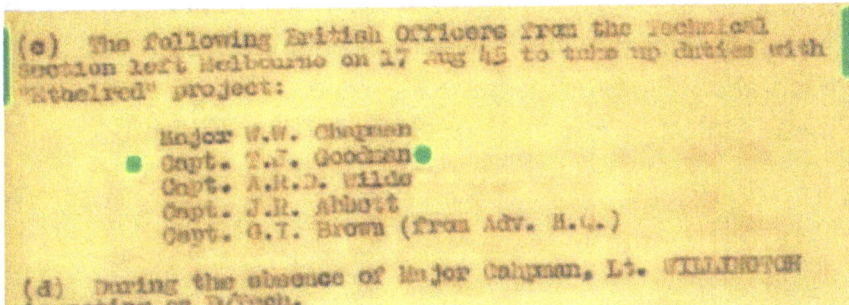

Figure 78

So, it was just two days later after the Japanese surrender, that Tom left S.R.D's HQ in Melbourne to join the British Pacific Fleet in Sydney harbour for *Operation Ethelred*. That Fleet was tasked to take back the British Colony of Hong Kong from the occupying Japanese Army there, which had not yet surrendered. This 'no surrender' stance of the Japanese military was not untypical as they considered surrender such a great loss of face that, if all else failed, suicide was a preferable fate. *Operation Ethelred* is thought to have been named that because the end of the War came so unexpectedly there was no time for proper preparation before *Ethelred* was embarked upon. This operation was also surrounded by the Allied political tensions of the immediate post war period, when it became obvious that China had an eye on absorbing the British colony back into her own territory and America's colonial views on restoring the British colony was not at all clear.

I also found references to Tom's S.R.D. presence in a rare Australian publication called *"They Came Unseen – The Men and Women of Z Force Special Unit"*. My ex-pat. friend (Paul Sansom) who lives in Rosemount, Queensland, managed to obtain a loan copy from his public library. Tom is listed, along with his service number and the entry *"Operation Ethelred"* it gave the date of his joining (TOS = Taken On Strength) as 4th April 1945. (Figs 79 & 80)

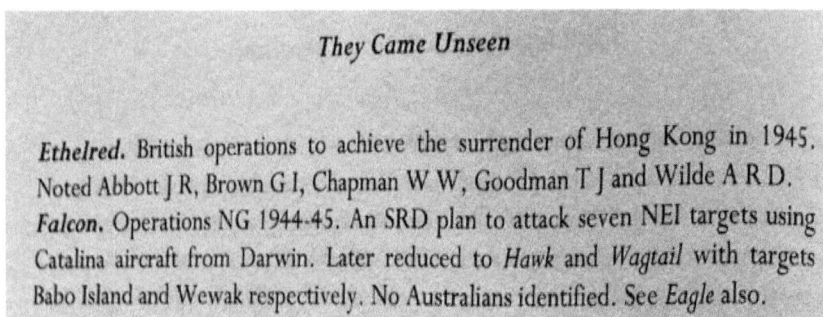

They Came Unseen

Ethelred. British operations to achieve the surrender of Hong Kong in 1945. Noted Abbott J R, Brown G I, Chapman W W, Goodman T J and Wilde A R D.
Falcon. Operations NG 1944-45. An SRD plan to attack seven NEI targets using Catalina aircraft from Darwin. Later reduced to *Hawk* and *Wagtail* with targets Babo Island and Wewak respectively. No Australians identified. See *Eagle* also.

Figure 79

				Ops from 1 May 45.
VB2343530, AKS 246	Sig	Goodman	L	Brit. SOS 9 Jul 45
VB173594, AKX 197	Capt	Goodman	T J	Brit. RE. TOS 4 Apr 45. Ops *Ethelred*. *
VX88977, AKV 170	Pte	Goodwin	Ernest A	Ops Darwin. From 19 MG Bn 27 May 44. *

Figure 80

Note in Fig 80 the reference should be AKX 137 not AKX 197 ref NAA records (Fig 73). and the further date disparity between the NAA records and Tom's Australian Army Service booklet, the latter which records his joining date as 10th July 1945. (Fig 72)

HMS *Anson* at Devonport, March 1945

Figure 81

On 29th August 1945, the British Pacific Fleet arrived off Hong Kong, headed by the Battleship Anson (Fig 81), along with Aircraft carriers HMS Indomitable, HMS Venerable and 19 other ships. The fleet sailed into Hong Kong harbour, but it is not known on which of the ships Tom had embarked for the Operation.

There is also no record of what Tom's specific task was on Operation Ethelred. However, given his background in Bomb Disposal and S.O.E., it is highly likely that he was going to be involved in disarming the retreating Japanese army's booby traps and mine fields. The Royal Engineers usually led where others followed – Ubique ! Operation Ethelred lasted for two weeks, during which there was house to house fighting before the Japanese occupiers finally surrendered. The S.O.E. interest group's earlier reference to Welfreighters being used in Hong Kong to ferry repatriated ex-POWs out to hospital vessels, is a further clue to Tom's possible involvement on that Operation.

Tom's Army service record (including form BR199A) also includes references to *"knowledge of..... Philippine Islands, (Palau Islands), Formosa* (Taiwan)*, China, French Indio-China* (Cambodia/Vietnam) *and New Guinea on Military Duties with M.O.I.(SP)"*. (Fig 82)

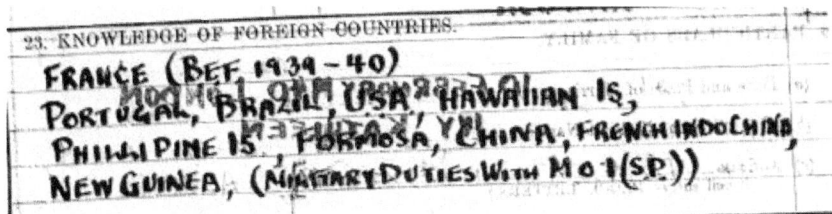

Figure 82

The Republic of Palau is a small island group in the western end of modern Micronesia. Generally speaking, it is north of the Vogelkop Peninsula of Irian Jaya and east of the Philippines island of Mindanao. (Fig 83)

The Palau islands were occupied by Japanese forces during WW2 and used to support its 1941 invasion of the Philippines, which succeeded in 1942. The invasion overthrew the American-installed Commonwealth government in the Philippines and installed the Japanese-backed Second Philippine Republic in 1943. The United States took the Palau Islands back from Japan in 1944 after the costly Battle of Peleliu,

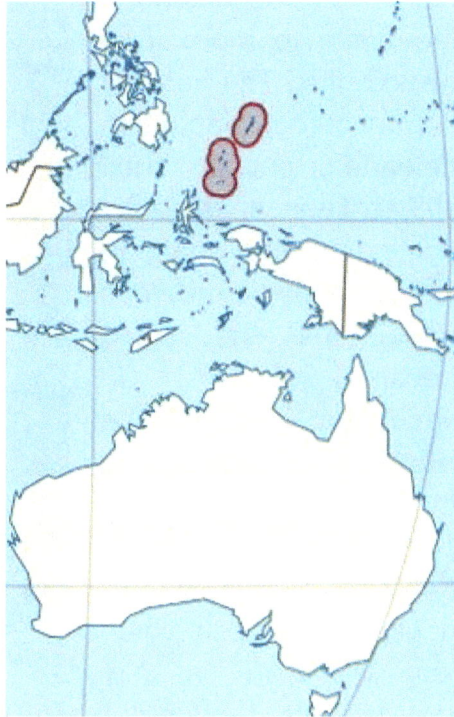

Figure 83

when more than 2,000 Americans and 10,000 Japanese were killed. US Marines of the 1st Marine Division and then soldiers of the US Army's 81st Infantry Division fought to capture the airfield on the small coral island of Peleliu. The battle was part of a larger offensive campaign known as Operation Forager, which ran from June to November 1944 in the Pacific Theatre. Major General William Rupertus, the commander of the 1st Marine Division, predicted that the island would be secured within four days. However, after repeated Imperial Japanese Army defeats in previous island campaigns, Japan had developed new island defence tactics and well-crafted fortifications, which allowed stiff resistance and extended the battle to more than two months. The heavily-outnumbered Japanese defenders put up such stiff resistance, often by fighting to the death in the Japanese Emperor's name, that the island became known in Japanese as the "Emperor's Island." In the US, it was a controversial battle because of the island's negligible strategic value and the high casualty

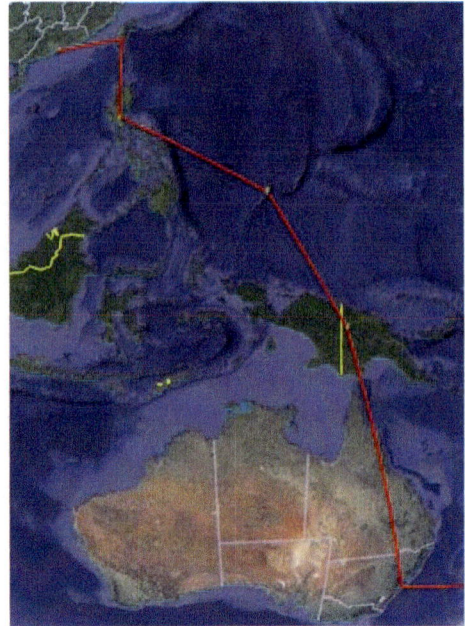
Figure 84

rate, which exceeded that of all other amphibious operations during the Pacific War. The National Museum of the Marine Corps called it "the bitterest battle of the war for the Marines". In 1945–1946, the United States re-established control of the Philippines and managed Palau through the Philippine capital of Manila. They established a Naval base on Palau after VJ day and used it as a POW repatriation staging camp.

After the Japanese surrender, a special Australian Intelligence Bureau (A.I.B.) P.O.W. interview team was formed (RAAF group 493). It also had a British section (No 3 British P.O.W. Reception Team) in which some British members of S.R.D. volunteered to serve. They assisted with interviews for the repatriation of Indian Army P.O.Ws. The structure and details of this short lived reception team does not appear to have been formally recorded, so the details of who and what the volunteers encountered remains unknown. Given Tom's disposition, it would not have been out of character for him to have volunteered for this role and there is no other known reason for him to have been in this remote region, other than to have been a member of S.R.D.'s team that is known to have joined the British Reception team.

The other locations mentioned in this section of Tom's Service Records are mapped in (Fig 84). Despite some serious endeavours, it has not been possible to unearth any specific leads that might explain exactly what he had been involved in at all the locations mentioned, apart from the Palau Islands. After plotting the places mentioned in his file ,on the map, it seems highly likely that they were probably on his route back to Australia, after the conclusion of Operation Ethelred. His passage would have been taken either by air transport or upon the decks of the British Pacific Fleet, or perhaps a combination of these ? In all, there was a period of approximately 14 weeks between the end of Operation Ethelred and Tom's recorded return the UK. At this point there is a date difference with regard to Tom's whereabouts at the end of WW2, following Operation Ethelred in August 1945. The M.O.D's military history, form BR199A, records Tom as returning to the UK in December 1945. His Australian Army Service book records two separate, hand stamped, inoculation entries (Tetanus and

Typhoid) by "Capt. P. Hanford R.A.M.C." dated 9th October 1946. (Fig 85)

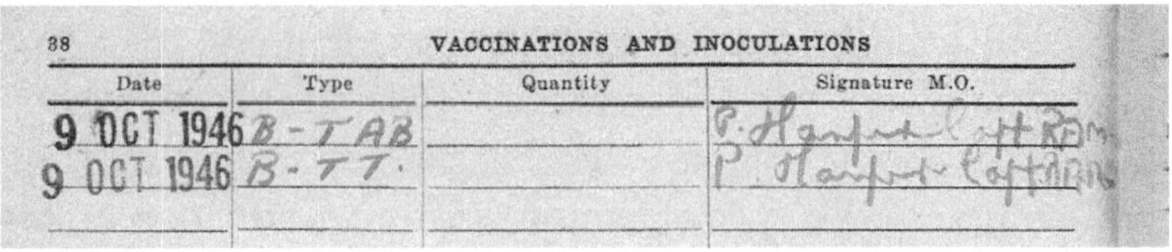

38	VACCINATIONS AND INOCULATIONS		
Date	Type	Quantity	Signature M.O.
9 OCT 1946	B - T AB		P. Hanford Ht RDM
9 OCT 1946	B - T T .		P. Hanford Captain

Figure 85

However, it is evident that the inoculation date stamps (year) in his Service book were incorrect and that they should in fact have been recorded as being administered on 9th October 1945.

One thing that has fallen into place, since researching Tom's military history, is the origin of a stuffed Kola bear skin that used to adorn our hallway table in Holdenby Road and also Chiswick. It was clearly a souvenir that Tom brought back from Australia on his way home from the War. Over the years it became increasing battered and worn, as it was frequently played with by the family. Eventually, the wood shaving stuffing simply turned to dust and it was consigned to the dustbin in the mid 1990s. Had I realised……….

Chapter 7 - Post War Bomb Disposal

So, Tom returned to the UK on 4th December 1945, he was again posted to R.E. Depot, Halifax (the R.E. holding station). He was *"Struck off Strength of M.O.I.(S.P.)"* on 31st December 1945 and reverted to *"remuneration from Army funds"*. No other details of Tom's deployment are shown at this point.

However, several books about WW2 Bomb Disposal have been written by Lt. Colonel Eric E. Wakeling. Two of these, *The Lonely War* (1994) and *The Danger of UXBs* (1996) throw some direct light on Tom's post War activity.

Lt. Col. Wakeling (centre Fig 86), who was then a Lieutenant), writes that in 1946 he was *"posted to*

Figure 86

No12 B.D Company on 15th March 1946 to be 2nd in command of that unit, under Major (Tom) John Goodman." He records that the Officers' Mess was the small *"cosy"* lodge of a large country estate's house. He (Wakeling) *"...had to share a small bedroom with George Churchill and his night & morning smoking routine"*. The O.C. (Tom) had his own room".

103

B.D. Company No. 12 was based in Horsham, covering Sussex and it's coastline. The B.D. Depot which housed the stores and "other ranks" was located close to Horsham town centre, at Caffyns Garage, in North Street. That building no longer exists and the site is now buried under the town's large Sainsbury's store.

Figure 87

The Lodge, that was the Officer's Mess and lodgings, is almost certainly the gate house of Denne House, which stands less than a mile south of the Depot site in Horsham, on the Worthing Road (B2237) (Fig 87). From Lt. Col. Wakeling's own writings, it would appear that life in B.D. at Horsham was not too taxing and there was ample time for 'relaxation' He recalled, *"The set up of just Major (Tom) John Goodman, George Churchill and I living in the mess at the Lodge, with the sections spread out around Sussex lasted for just three months.*

But it was an enjoyable time, having the odd trip out in the evening to a local pub and on a Saturday or Sunday afternoon nipping down to Brighton, in an Army vehicle of course. Actually, the O.C. (Tom) had a Vauxhall Car as his vehicle, so we travelled

Figure 88

*in comfort. We were "visiting the stores unit at Shoreham", if we were ever stopped by the Military Police!" (*Fig 88)

Apart from dealing with German UXBs, No 12 B.D. Company was also involved in clearing the British defensive minefields that had been laid along the Sussex coastline, including Brighton and Shoreham. Such mine clearance was quite hazardous as, although the location of the mines had been recorded when they were laid on the beaches during the hostilities, the tides had caused the shingle and sand to move about - taking the mines with them ! So, it required some invention to come up with a safe way to reveal where they had been re-distributed. A high pressure water cannon was the solution they came up with which was used to blast away the shingle and sand to expose the mines. (Fig 89)

By 1948 only three known coastal minefields were left uncleared at Hastings, Folkestone and Mundesley (Norfolk).

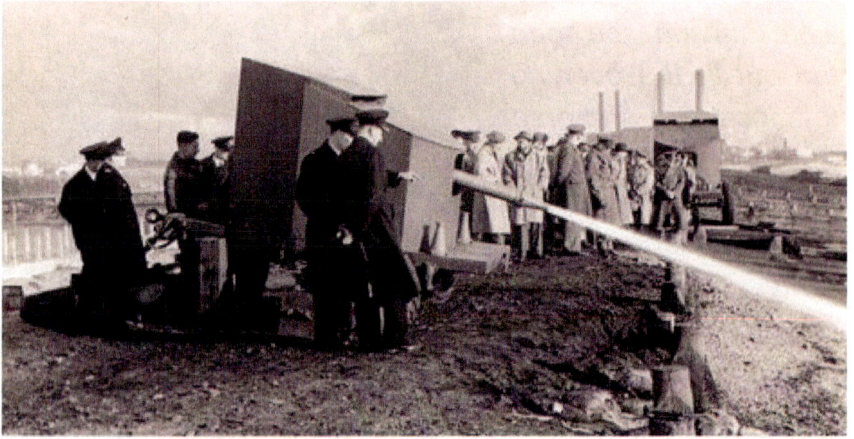

Figure 89

B.D. Company No. 12 was disbanded on 15th June 1946. Lt. Col. Wakeling recounted, "......we *had a great farewell party at the Lodge. The Chief Royal Engineer came over for the party and left having bought the carpet in the ante-room of the Mess. I came away with the cutlery. It was a sad day on the morning after the party. We all went our different ways. Major Goodman was going to another command where the O.C. had been de-mobbed.*"

There is a corner of the Horsham cemetery that is devoted to the Officers and men of No 12 B.D. Company who were killed whilst serving there.

Post WW2, the Horsham B.D. depot became the Army's School of Bomb Disposal for all bomb disposal troops in the UK's three armed services. They also trained similar forces from many other countries. The facilities there included three buildings where examples were displayed of every type of missile and bomb dropped on the UK in WW2, together with examples of our own landmines and bombs. Also on display was the equipment used to disarm them, including Canadian Diamond Drilling equipment. The display also included two V1s, a conventional one (unmanned) and a piloted version (Fig 90) where the pilot could guide it to the target leaving at

Figure 90

the last minute by parachute. There was also an example of a V2 rocket in the collection.

I had a tip off from my friend, John Friberg, who had also been in the R.E.s, about the existence of the book "*Danger*

Figure 91

UXB" by Lt. Col Wakeling (Fig 91), I traced him via his publisher and it was in June 1997 that Margaret and I went to meet him at his house in Bourne End, Buckinghamshire. Beforehand, I had explained on the 'phone who I was and that I believed my Father had been his C.O. at one time, post war. When we arrived to meet him, Lt Col. Wakeling opened his front door and exclaimed "*Hello, no mistaking the mould you came from – do come in !*". He was quite right, I do bear a close visual resemblance to my Father. We spent all too short a time talking about his work with Tom. After some tea, I purchased a copy of his second book *Danger UXBs,* which he kindly inscribed. I had intended to return to talk more about his time working with Tom, but somehow it escaped me and life got in the way yet again. At the age of 21, in June 1943, the then Lieutenant Wakeling, was a section commander serving with 3 B.D. Company in Nottingham. He had the dubious honour of having to deal with more than 2,000 German SD2 anti-personnel mines that had rained down on Grimsby and Cleethorpes. Though the Luftwaffe employed a range of anti-personnel bombs, the SD2 was used just once on a large scale against the UK. It was the so-called Butterfly Bomb. (Fig 92)

These 2kg bombs were dropped in cylindrical containers that held 23 bombs, or more. Once dropped the containers were blown open by an air burst fuze scattering the SD2s far & wide. As the bombs fell from the container, their outer case was flicked open by springs that caused four light metal drogues to deploy, with a protruding 5 inch steel cable, in the form of a parachute & wind

Figure 92

vane. As this vane rotated it moved up the cable. That action turned the spindle which was screwed into the fuze as a safety device, thus arming the bomb. The Germans had not dropped these devices in such numbers before.

They caused absolute havoc and, literally, brought Grimsby to a stand still. It took 3 months to clear the town and surrounding area of these mines. Because of the havoc the Butterfly Bomb raid caused, the incident was 'hushed up' so that the Germans did not learn how effective the deployment had been and so it was never repeated on that scale. This raid also formed the basis for an episode of the 1970s TV series, Danger UXB, starring Anthony Andrews.

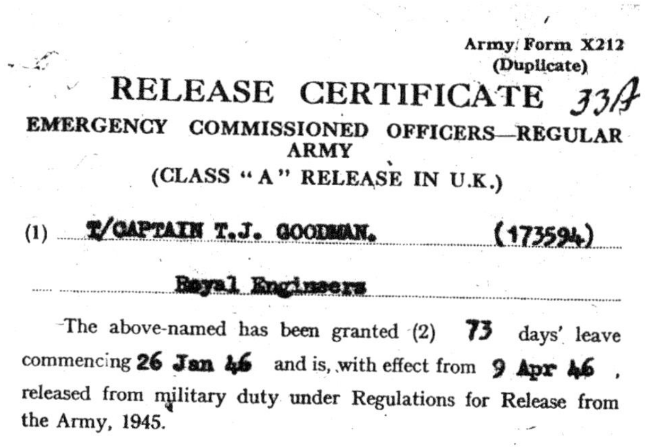

Lt Col. Wakeling was demobilised in 1947 and retired

Army Form X212
(Duplicate)

RELEASE CERTIFICATE 33/A

EMERGENCY COMMISSIONED OFFICERS—REGULAR ARMY

(CLASS " A " RELEASE IN U.K.)

(1) T/CAPTAIN T.J. GOODMAN. (173594)

Royal Engineers

The above-named has been granted (2) **73** days' leave commencing **26 Jan 46** and is, with effect from **9 Apr 46**, released from military duty under Regulations for Release from the Army, 1945.

Figure 93

from civilian working life in 1967. He was a founder member and Secretary of the Royal Engineers Bomb Disposal Club. He died in Kent on 11th November 2013.

There is a slight discrepancy between the dates quoted by Lt Col Wakeling as to when he was my Father's No 2 and those on Tom's Service record. The MOD's records (Fig 93) show that Tom went on pre-release leave at home, in Brockley, from 26th January 1946 to 8th April 1946, when he was then 'Class A' released from the Army on 9th April 1946.

As has been discovered, the records don't always reflect what actually happened. This was probably because there were so many staff movements going on at the time and I think Tom was keen to remain with The Colours that he would have taken almost any posting to remain with The R.E's. It does look as if Tom was "demobbed" and integrated into the Army reserve, for recall.

However, only a trip to the National Archives at Kew and sight of No 12 B.D. Company's Unit's Diaries might solve that question, if they still exist. Either way, there is no doubt that Tom was in bomb disposal after the War and he certainly was Lieutenant Wakeling's C.O. in 1946.

During his "pre-release leave", Tom had looked for work in "civvy street". It would have been a time when many of thousands of men and women were returning home to be de-mobbed from their wartime military service and seeking their re-employment in civvy street. Inevitably, jobs were as scarce then as they were back in the great depression of 1929, that Tom, and the Goodman family, had endured. In a letter to Tom, dated 2nd August 1945, from a contact named E. Ramsay-Green of the *Navy and Military Club* in Piccadilly, it was suggested that "*without any promises, he may be able to fix something up* (for Tom)". On that letter, my father had annotated '*Mr Sutton, Mayfair 7074, Bank of N.S.W., Berkley Square - Mail Section ?*'. I conclude that Tom had his sights on better things. Quite how long it was before he received this letter is unknown, as Tom was definitely in Australia at the time of its writing.

Tom's Army service record (form B199A) notes that he worked as "*Chief Assistant to Mg G J Sutton, MI Mech E,*

Consulting Engineer, 32 Old Queen Street, London SW1, designing Special Purpose Industrial Machinery 1945-46".

Again, nothing definite is known about his role in that job. However, I do have a recollection that my Father mentioned that he had once been involved with designing some commercial machines, including one that "... *put the blobs on the ends of ladies hair clips".* I can only assume that this job would not have held the same degree of interest and scope for him, as did his army service. So, not surprisingly it wasn't very long before he re-applied to the Army for a Commission.

Today, that Queen Street London address is valued as the second most expensive in SW1, at £13.2m. (Fig 94).

Figure 94

Chapter 8 - Special Forces Club

Before his planned demob, Tom joined the Special Forces Club (S.F.C.) on 14th March 1946. I presume he did so as a means of making contact with other like minded individuals and to explore the possibilities for future postings in the Army or perhaps out in "civvy Street". For the princely sum of 5 Guineas (£270 today) he became 'Life Member No 1088'. (Fig 95)

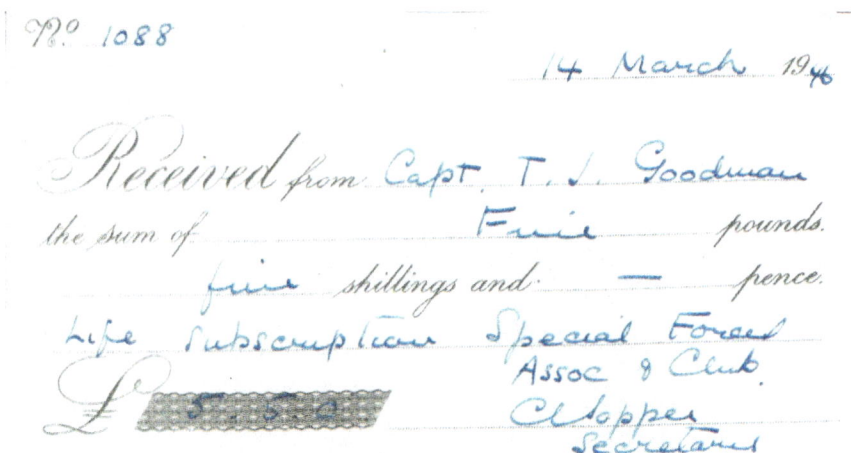

Figure 95

The S.F.C. is an extremely exclusive and very low profile organisation that is located in the quieter, leafy, streets of Knightsbridge in London. It was founded by Major General Sir Colin Gubbins, the last Chief of the Special Operations Executive, in 1945.

The object of the club was *"to establish a Club which would be of direct practical and immediate benefit to the younger members of SOE, men and women who had joined us during the war and who at the end of it had to start a completely new life in a strange and upset world."*

The club was a meeting place, exclusively, for ex S.O.E. agents, personnel and Resistance members from all over the World, be they men or women of any rank, reflecting the membership and spirit of the SOE. Membership gave them the right to stay at the club overnight for a modest charge. Those modest charges continue to this day.

Through a contact I made in 2022, when researching S.O.E. at Tangmere Military Aviation Museum, I was lucky enough to be introduced to a current member of the S.F.C. who invited me there for luncheon, with himself and two of his friends. It was quite emotional to think I was going to be walking in the footsteps of my father, who had frequented that building almost 80 years beforehand (Fig 96).

Figure 96

I know that Tom would have enjoyed a dram, or two, in the members bar for, in those days, he did like "*a drop of Scotch*" from time to time. Given its exclusive nature, I was amazed to find that the food and beverage prices at S.F.C. were so remarkably reasonable. Previous references, in the public domain, to the Club's *"threadbare carpet and poor state of decoration"* are certainly no longer relevant. The Club has recently been very tastefully re-decorated and furnished. It also has elaborate measures of protection against intrusion and external assault, because of the constituent nature of the membership.

There is an interesting photographic portrait gallery on the staircase honouring the most prominent S.F.C. members. Those who were killed in action are framed in black. Almost all the WW2 figures in that collection are field agents. Being one of the 'backroom boffins', my Father is not amongst them.

Today, the club's membership is drawn primarily from the intelligence / security communities, both military and civilian, and Special Forces along with other organisations and individuals whose work reflects the ethos of the club, such as high-threat bomb disposal experts and members drawn from the *"psyops"* community. Great stress is placed on the personal qualities of applicants, along with their technical qualifications, to ensure that the club maintains its reputation as one of the most discreet locations in London.

The current membership of S.F.C. includes those esteemed holders of the Victoria Cross and George Cross.

Chapter 9 - PYTHON, India & Singapore I

So, it was on 24th September 1946 that Tom re-joined the colours (initially as a Lieutenant) and was posted to R.E Depot, on a Short Service Commission for 7 years. Soon after rejoining The

Figure 97

Colours, he embarked an unknown troop ship for India on 22nd October 1946, dis-embarking at Bombay on 8th November 1946 Almost certainly Tom would have landed in sight of India Gate (Fig 97). In India, he was to join the Head Quarters, Regimental Centre, Royal Indian Engineers, with the resumed rank of Captain. Soon after, on that posting, he became Acting Major, then Temporary Major.

India Gate was built on the waterfront at Bombay (Mumbai) to commemorate the landing of King George V in 1911, when he arrived for his Coronation as Emperor of India. The foundation stone was laid in 1913 and the Gate was finally completed in 1924. However, The King only saw a cardboard model of what was to be built.

In February 1946, a Royal Indian Navy uprising had taken place in Bombay against the British Government's rule in India. It had spread across the Indian sub-continent and ended up involving over 20,000 sailors and 78 ships. That mutiny had started in connection with sailors' general post war living conditions and poor food-stuffs. It was one of the events that culminated in India gaining its independence from British Rule, in August 1947.

Not long after Tom's arrival in India, a further posting arose for him with the Chief Engineer, Asia Land Forces, South East Asia. After only five months, in March 1947, Tom was promoted to full Major and appointed Deputy Assistant Director of Engineering Services, General Headquarters, South East Asian Land Forces, Singapore.

He subsequently *"emplaned Singapore for duty in Hong Kong, 20th December 1947"* where he was for 4 days before returning to Singapore and then back to the UK. for *"T/Duty attached to D.E.S. War Office for Liaison Visit for period 23 March to 23 April 1948"*. The destination and subject of that Liaison visit is not known, but it could well be related to the *'deferment'* that follows later on his record.

Tom actually returned to Singapore on 22nd April 1948, joining the Director of Engineering Services (D.E.S) staff. He was accompanied on that posting by my Mother (Ivy) and elder brother. They lived in the Alexandra Married Quarters at 3B Berkshire Road. At the time, my mother was pregnant with my sister Sylvia, who was born in the British Military Hospital Alexandra on 18th July 1948. Sylvia died just 4 days later

GOODMAN T J
SYLVIA MARGARET DAUGHTER OF
MAJOR 173391 GHO FARELF
27 JULY 1949

Figure 98

116

and is now buried in the Military section of the Kranji War Graves Cemetery (Fig 98) a short distance from the Causeway Bridge across to the Malay peninsula. Originally, she was laid to rest in the British Military Cemetery, Dover Road. However, that location was re-developed in the 1980s and all its burial plots were moved to the Kranji War Graves Cemetery.

Whilst stationed in Singapore, Tom submitted his design for a *"Tractor Drawn, Power Operated, Root Extractor".* His specification and drawings were dated 11th April 1949. (Fig 99) It was a suggestion he put forward to assist The Overseas Food Corporation (O.F.C.) at Kongwa, Tanganyika Territory who were clearing land to grow Ground

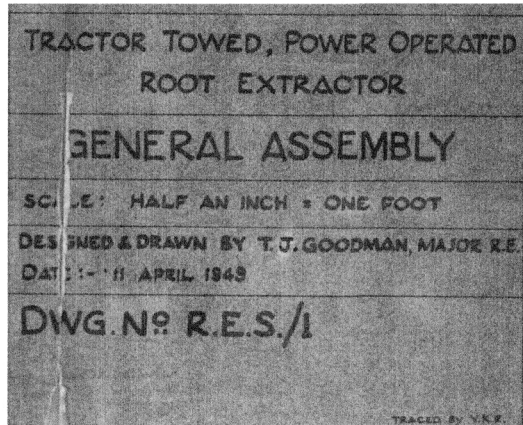

Figure 99

Nuts and for other agricultural purposes. Tom's design and drawings for this machine were completed in his own hand. It was described by Mr K. Pennycuick, Director, Operation Research Unit, OFC as *"a very ingenious implement"* (sic). However, it was considered, overall, that *"… the power plant (tractor) required to operate it would make it uneconomic".* So, they retained an American equivalent manufactured by Blaw-Knox !

Tom came up with a further design that was for *"A Prefabricated, Aluminium Landing Mat" (P.A.L.M.)* which was submitted to the Chief Engineer, Far Eastern Land Forces in 1949. It was intended *"To provide a means of constructing TAF Fighter and Bomber Landing Mats or Re-fuelling and Re-arming strips much more rapidly on low grade soils than is possible with the methods at present in use."* Tom had several of his *P.A.L.M. Mats* made at ¼ scale, for demonstration purposes (Fig 99a). For some unknown reason, the submission was 'buried' in the War Office for five years before Tom was able to resurrect the subject with Brigadier E. Myers, in Moascar, Egypt in January 1956. A further 2 years elapsed before the Ministry of Supply provided the official comment *"An*

Figure 99a

interesting paper...... but the weight exceeds the present ideas for a lightweight prefabricated surface". Seven years after its first submission, the Ministry of Supply again decided to remain using an American manufactured alternative ! Much to my Mother's annoyance, the Landing Mat samples adorned a corner of our passageway at 35A Holdenby Road, in Brockley, until the family moved to Chiswick in 1966, when they were finally "let go".

Tom's record notes *"approval for deferment PYTHON for 6 months to October 1949."* In fact, his tenure on this tour of Singapore lasted until 27th April 1950 when he returned to the U.K. with the family. (At the time of their return, my mother was pregnant with me, to be born in September 1950.)

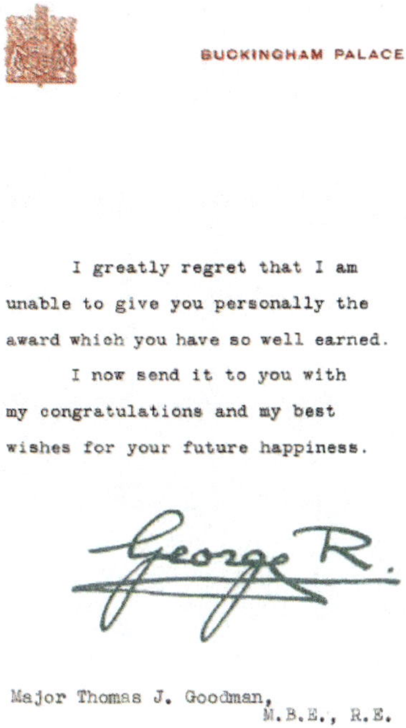

Following a recommendation by the Commander in Chief, Far Eastern Land Forces, Tom was awarded the M.B.E. (Military) in May 1950. This

BUCKINGHAM PALACE

I greatly regret that I am unable to give you personally the award which you have so well earned.

I now send it to you with my congratulations and my best wishes for your future happiness.

George R.

Major Thomas J. Goodman, M.B.E., R.E.

Figure 100

was announced in the London Gazette on 16th May 1950. Unfortunately, Tom's return to the UK from Singapore coincided with this award. There was some confusion as to where the Medal and paperwork should be sent for presentation. They actually sent it to Singapore. By the time it arrived, Tom and the family was already in transit back to the UK. It was then held up in Singapore's bureaucracy before being sent back to the UK, missing the presentation ceremony window. So, the opportunity for my Mother to have a *"new hat"* for the presentation by The King was missed. However, King George VI wrote to him, in absentia, with his congratulations. (Fig 100)

I recall Tom telling me, *"your mother cried her eyes out when we first arrived in Singapore because she was home-sick for her brothers, sisters and widowed Mother…"*

Figure 101

(by 1950, Ivy's mother was becoming quite frail and immobile. Having suffered from Polio, Granny Waters required a leg calliper to help her get about.) "…..*however, after a couple of months she got used to having domestic servants, including a cook, an Amah to look after your* (my) *brother and a handyman gardener to tend around the house. It meant she was free to go about as she pleased, to enjoy Canasta and coffee mornings with the other Army wives (Fig 101). So, when it was time to return to the UK, and back into normal domestic life at 35A Holdenby Road, she cried her eyes out to go back to Singapore again."*

Figure 102

Tom joined the PYTHON project once he was back in the UK, on 27th April 1950. (Fig 102) PYTHON is a highly effective minefield clearance system that has been used by the British Army since the 1950's. It is a trailer mounted system that is towed by an armoured vehicle, typically a tank. PYTHON fires a rocket that is attached to a 230m long hose packed with one and a half tons of high explosive. When the hose lands on the ground it explodes and destroys, or clears, 90% of the mines along its length. It was developed from the Giant Viper system (which is a later version of the CONGER system) that was deployed for a short time in 1944, but with the more stable PE4 high explosive making it a very effective weapon. The Giant Viper was designed to clear a path through minefields approximately the width of a tank. It launched a cluster of eight solid fuel rockets which pulled a plastic hose filled with 1500kg of PE4 explosive over the area to be cleared.

After landing, and when clear of the launching vehicle, the PE4 is then detonated. Usually an Armoured Vehicle Royal Engineers (AVRE) is the first vehicle to enter the newly formed gap in the minefield equipped with a bull dozer blade to prepare the route for following vehicles. The early version of Giant Viper could also be towed

Figure 103

by an armoured personnel carrier, using a special drawbar. (Fig 103) PYTHON was used during combat operations in Afghanistan, in February 2010. Royal Engineers fired the PYTHON rocket-powered mine clearance system to blow up improvised explosive devices (IEDs) lined along a route in Helmand Province as part of Operation Moshtarak. It was also used to clear a dry river bed of IEDs north of Patrol Base Wahid in Nad-e-Ali district in Helmand.(Fig 104)

Figure 104

After PYTHON, and a brief period on the 'Pool Staff ' at RE Depot, Tom was posted to No1 Engineering Stores Depot

(E.S.D), Long Marston and subsequently appointed Officer Commanding Headquarters Squadron, No 1 E.S.D. Long Marston, on 18th August 1950.

The village of Long Marston lies three miles south west of Stratford-upon-Avon. In 1859 the Oxford Worcester and Wolverhampton railway opened a branch line from Honeybourne to Stratford-upon-Avon and the station at Long Marston came into operation as one of the stops on the line. In early 1951, whilst Tom was stationed back at Long Marston, preparations were in hand for the Festival of Britain on the South Bank of the Thames.

As part of those preparations, the Royal Engineers were building one of their Bailey Bridges as a pedestrian walkway alongside Charing Cross Bridge (otherwise known as Hungerford Bridge) to enable

Figure 105

the mass of expected foot visitors to cross the Thames directly to the Exhibition site on the South Bank, from the Northern side. During the building of that Bailey footbridge some difficulties were encountered in placing the very long spans into position onto the temporary piers. There was an incident where one of the spans was actually dropped into The Thames and reported in the National Press. Tom was

123

sent down to London, from Long Marston, to assist in the temporary bridge construction.

The photograph (Fig 105) was taken during his site visit and it was amongst the few items found in his document case.

The Coronation of Queen Elizabeth II took place in June 1953. Tom's Plant Troop was chosen to be involved in the Coronation ceremonies. The photo at (Fig 106) was taken at their barracks, in London, in the morning, before the Troop

Figure 106

left to take up their positions. Tom (seated middle front row) was awarded the Queen's Coronation medal for his part in the proceedings. By all accounts, Coronation day 1953 was quite a rainy day, so perhaps it was due reward for getting soaked to the skin . He is centre front, 'swagger stick across his knees.

Chapter 10 - Egypt & Suez

The Suez Canal was an economically and strategically vital route for both Middle Eastern oil and trade with the Far East. Britain maintained a military presence in Egypt to protect the canal under the terms of a treaty signed in 1936. However, Egyptian nationalists resented the British presence in their country. As early as 1945, riots broke out and the first British soldier was killed. An operation to disarm the police in Ismailia in January 1952 resulted in the deaths of 40 Egyptian paramilitaries, and the death and wounding of several British soldiers.

It was on 18th April 1954 that Tom flew to Egypt and was '*Taken on the Strength*' (TOS) of the R.E. Works Establishment, Middle Eastern Land Forces Egypt, as O.C. No 1 E.S.D. Plant

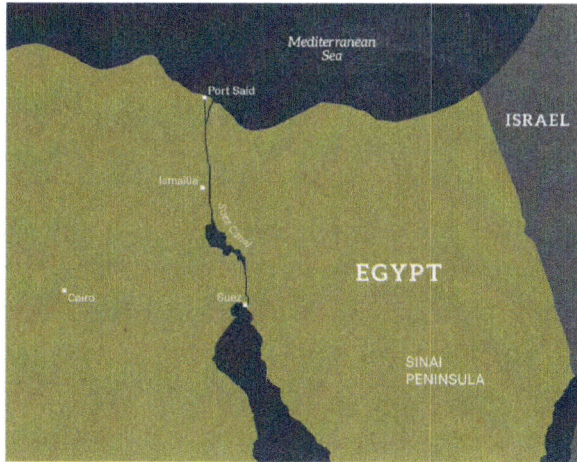

Figure 107

Troop. He was based in the Canal Zone garrison town of Ismailia. (Fig 107)

In October 1954, Britain and Egypt had concluded an agreement on the evacuation of Britain's Canal Zone garrison. The treaty also stated that the Suez Canal Company would not transfer to Egyptian government control until 1968. President Nasser's actions were an increasing threat to both British and French interests in the region. The two countries agreed that if no progress could be made at the negotiating table, they would send a force to occupy the canal and, if necessary, overthrow Nasser. France also wanted rid of Nasser as he was supporting rebels who were trying to overthrow French rule in Algeria. Withdrawing from the cities, British forces concentrated in the area immediately adjacent to the canal, known as 'the Canal Zone'. Then, in October 1951, the Egyptian government increased pressure on the British and repealed the 1936 treaty. Between 1950 and 1956, violence escalated: 54 servicemen were killed and many others injured.

Back in the U.K., my sister Kathleen was born in February 1954. When she was 6 months old she became ill. My mother was very concerned about her condition and summoned my paternal grandmother (Tom's mother, Gwendoline) for advice. I recall Gwendoline saying *"quick, call the doctor"*. It transpired that Kathleen had contracted Diphtheria, a highly contagious bacterial infection of the throat. She was gravely ill. Tom was *'returned to home establishment'* on compassionate leave, from Egypt, on 8th August 1954. Nine days later, I went with them both to visit Kathleen in Lewisham Hospital. As they went into the hospital to see her, I was left in the care of the hospital's gate keeper. We sat in his gatehouse by a coke fired brazier, just like the ones they used to roast chestnuts on in Oxford Street. When my parents returned to collect me a while later they were visibly upset. Kathleen had died. She was the second daughter they had lost and I know that my parents had really hoped for a daughter. That was the night of 17th August 1954.

Hansard records and reports all the U.K. Parliament's official debates. It records that, in 1954, amongst children under 1 year, there were only 36 notified Diphtheria cases and just 4 deaths from it.

Tom was temporarily assigned to the War Office, in the immediate aftermath of Kathleen's death, before being posted back to Egypt, this time taking our family with him, including myself. We left Crofton Park, in south east London, bound for Egypt on 24th November 1954. I clearly recall travelling to Heathrow Airport in a black cab, where we alighted next to several large marquees. Close by, we could see our aircraft parked on an apron next to the runway. It was an Avro 685 York. (Fig 108)

Figure 108

The Avro York passenger 'plane was based on the famous WW2 Lancaster bomber. It featured a high wing mounted on a new square-section boxy fuselage with a considerably increased internal volume when compared with the Avro 683 Lancaster bomber. The first two prototypes had twin fins (as did the Lancaster) but all subsequent aircraft were fitted with a third central fin to improve directional stability. In total, some 46 ex-RAF aircraft were ultimately transferred for civil use, many of them being subsequently used on trooping contracts. Only two examples of the Avro York aircraft remain today. One is at the Imperial War Museum at Duxford the other at the RAF Museum, Cosford.

Never glamorous, the Avro 685 York was widely used by a number of post-war airlines including BOAC and Dan Air. My abiding memory is the noise made by the four piston engines. They were so loud it was almost impossible to hold a conversation with the seats behind, where my parents were seated. (I did wonder whether the boiled sweets offered by the cabin crew before take off would have been more productive stuck in my ears, rather than sucked to help offset the change in cabin pressure).

As far as I recall, we made the journey to Egypt non-stop, which seems to agree with the York's maximum range of 4,800 km, against the distance from London to Cairo of 3,500km. However, I cannot actually recall which airfield we landed at. It could possibly have been RAF Fayid, which was the main transport staging post inside the Canal Zone. Either way, we were headed for Ismailia, which was also in the Canal Zone.

Our Married quarters were located on a Military estate. It was a bungalow with a fairly spacious, if sparsely planted and quite sandy garden, at 12 Southend Avenue, Ismailia. At the bottom of the garden there was a double fence, each 10ft high and spaced 10 feet apart, beyond them was desert. My mother's pride and joy in that garden were the sunflowers that grew and flowered at a great height. (Fig 109)

Figure 109

We had two domestic servants at the bungalow. Fadelia was our housekeeper / cook (Fig 110).

We also had a Gardener and handyman, whose name I

Figure 110

cannot now recall. (Fig 111)

Figure 111

Figure 112

Tom's new Egypt posting was to the R.E. Works Depot, in Moascar. I visited the Works Depot with him several times during our stay there. He is on the right in this photo, wearing his cap in (Fig 112). This picture was taken not long before the Suez crisis escalated.

I know that both my parents enjoyed their time in Egypt. It was a very busy working time for Tom, but they still found time to have fun with their friends. Two of whom they often partied with were identical twins and wealthy civilian businessmen. We once went sailing with them on their yacht on Lake Tismah, part of the Suez Canal, setting out from the Ismailia Yacht club which is on its western bank. I recall being terrified as the yacht heeled over, water up to the level of the gunnels, in a very strong afternoon breeze. This was probably the sort of afternoon desert wind that caused the container ship, Evergiven, to block the canal in 2021.

Here (Fig 113) Tom is at a Mess function, with the Twins, wearing his "No3 Warm Weather" mess dress. The No3 was adopted in the 1950s for units whilst based in tropical stations.

One afternoon, after school, Tom asked me if I would like to take a ride with him in his car, a black Ford Popular. He explained that two of his Sappers had been arrested by the Military Police, having been caught scaling a War Memorial. They had been "put on a charge" and he was having to decide what to do with them. So, he wanted to "visit the scene of the crime". I had often wondered exactly where that

Figure 113

memorial was but could not remember anything about it except that there were two tall towers on the banks of a waterway.

In 2013, whilst on a cruise that made a south to North transit of the Suez Canal we approached Ismailia. There, out of the desert heat haze, appeared a scene that took me back to that afternoon's ride with my Father. (Fig 114) The memorial turned out to be a commemoration of the defence of the Suez Canal in World

Figure 114

War 1. It was right on the banks of the canal itself. Around the same time, Tom took me to the Officers Mess for "*a glass of something*". My Mother inscribed on the rear of the picture "*We Three, Xmas 1955*".

(Fig 115)

Figure 115

Officers did not usually go to the Navy, Army, Air Force Institute (NAAFI) as the Officers Mess had its own, similar facilities. However, I recall that on one occasion we did go there for tea. It may have been at the invitation of one of Tom's staff who was leaving for the UK. It was funny to discover that there was a particular NAAFI currency, in the form of brass tea tokens and plastic ones in green and red. (Figs 116-118)

Figure 116

Figure 117

Figure 118

My Father's Ford Popular once carried us to see the Pyramids at Giza. (Fig 119) I recall how hot and dusty it was there. But it was nowhere near as built up then, as when I returned to re-visit the Pyramids in 2000. However, the Ford Popular didn't prove so popular on the way back ! We were driving back to Ismailia, not long after having crossed the River Nile, when there

Figure 119

was a loud 'graunching' sound from the rear of the vehicle. Tom pulled over to the kerb and we all got out. He said *"That's the end of that. The back axle has gone. The brakes were not very good anyway, so we'll leave it here and get a taxi the rest of the way home"* He told my Mother, *"After a few days, there will be nothing left of it as the Arabs are very good at recycling."*

In my Father's document bag, I also discovered that he had been issued with a 5 year passport at the British Consulate, Ismailia on 1st April 1955. It includes reference to a number of middle Eastern countries, but there are no entry / exit stamps to indicate if it was ever used ? It does not include entitlement for any of our family members on it. Perhaps this was for more covert activity. (Fig 120)

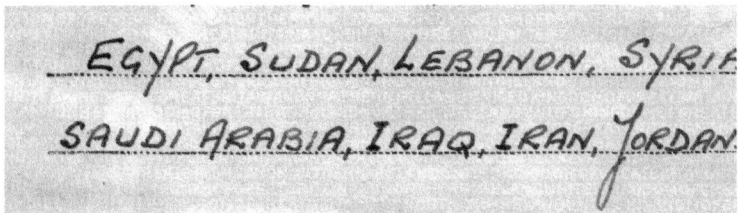

Figure 120

Not long before we departed from Egypt, the R.E. Works Depot was wound up. My father was responsible for organising the general auction sale to dispose of the stores' raw materials and equipment. I remember him saying at home after the sale had finished, that it was one of his saddest army days to see *"what a pittance"* was paid for the various sale Lots. Tom is wearing the cap in foreground, mid- left. (Fig 121)

Figure 121

Political tensions, over the Suez Canal, were rising in 1955 and there was an incident involving the bungalow next door to ours. One evening, in early 1956, there was a loud explosion which demolished the back of that property.

(Fig 122) A number of Army figures - "investigators" came to look through the rubble. I guess they were trying to work out what had caused it. The windows of all these bungalows had a fine mesh over them to keep out the biting bugs. I remember that, around the same time as that explosion, it was

Figure 122

discovered that the mesh over one of our own bungalow's windows had a hole bored in it, about an inch in diameter. Our parents didn't discuss the matter in front of us children, but there was definitely a heightened tension at home afterwards. I don't recall being privy to hearing what caused the explosion next door, but a few days after it we were evacuated from our quarters. Tom came home one afternoon and said *"just take what you can carry"*. All I was allowed to take was a small red toy attaché case containing my worldly possessions which amounted to some small toys and a length of silver Christmas tree tinsel. Some time later, the contents spilled out causing some hilarity to my parents and others nearby and a red face to me. We were transported, at speed in the back of an Army Land Rover, as part of a convoy across the desert. We arrived at a transit camp in Port Said at the Northern end of the Suez Canal,

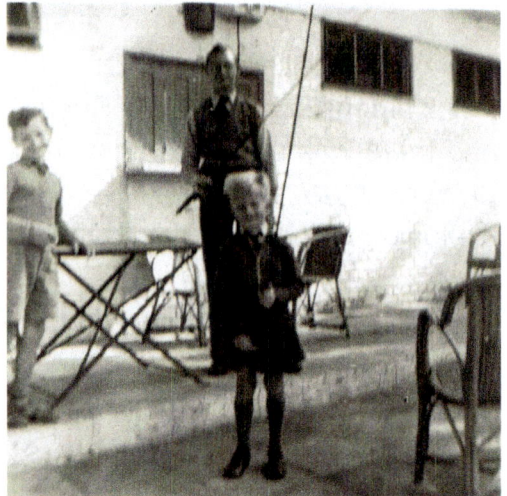

Figure 123

where quite a number of other service families were awaiting developments. There I had my first experience of fishing (Fig 123). Quite where the fishing waters were, I have no idea, but possibly the canal itself. We were held in that Transit camp for just over 2 weeks. My recollection of the camp is of crude accommodation buildings, quite cool evening temperatures and communal meals seated with a number of other army families under large army canvas bell tents.

On 16th March 1956 Tom was posted to the staff of the Chief Engineer (Singapore) and shortly after we boarded one of Her Majesty's troop ships, the SS Empire Fowey, at Port Said, bound for Singapore (Fig 124). We called en-route at Aden and Colombo. It was the SS Empire Fowey's Voyage No. 28, That voyage had a duration of six weeks from 22nd February to 21st March 1956. SS Empire Fowey had started

Figure 124

her six week voyage at Southampton and called in at Gibraltar and Algiers, before she arrived for us to embark at Port Said.

President Nasser nationalised the Suez Canal Company on 26 July 1956. Prior to that it was owned primarily by British and French shareholders. On 29 October, Israel invaded the

Egyptian Sinai. Britain and France issued a joint ultimatum to cease fire, which was ignored. On 5 November, Britain and France landed paratroopers along the Suez Canal. Before the Egyptian forces were defeated, they had blocked the canal to all shipping by sinking 40 ships in the canal. It later became clear that Israel, France and Britain had conspired to plan the invasion. The three allies had achieved a number of their military objectives, but the canal was rendered useless. Heavy political pressure from the United States and the USSR led to a withdrawal. U.S. president Dwight D. Eisenhower had given strongly warnings to Britain not to invade. He threatened serious damage to the British financial system by selling the U.S. government's pound sterling bonds. Historians conclude that crisis signified the end of Great Britain's role as one of the world's major powers. The Suez Canal was closed from October 1956 until March 1957.

Following a lengthy campaign, partly led by my friend and ex-Sapper John Friberg, Prime Minister Tony Blair announced on 11th June 2003 that the Committee on the Grant of Honours, Decorations and Medals had under consideration the case for recognition of service in the Suez Canal Zone between 1951 and 1954, with special regard to the hardships and dangers which accompanied duty there. The committee's

Figure 125

recommendations were duly submitted to The Queen who graciously approved the award of the General Service Medal (GSM) with clasp 'Canal Zone' (Fig 125).

The qualifying criteria were published in a Command Paper that was seen and approved by The Queen and laid before Parliament. Medals were to be issued by the Ministry of Defence medal offices. Veterans and their families were able to claim the award. Claims were checked against official records held by the department to confirm eligibility to the medal, or as instructed by the individual medal office. My claim for this to be awarded to Tom, posthumously, was approved. His GSM Canal Zone clasp was issued by the M.O.D. in December 2020. His name has also been added to the Roll of Honor on the "Canal Zoners" web site.

(Fig 126)

Figure 126

Chapter 11 Singapore II

En-route to Singapore we called into the ports of Aden, then a British Protectorate but now part of Yemen, and Colombo in Sri Lanka. On arrival at Colombo we took a taxi trip around the city and visited the Zoo which, compared to the standards of animal housing that exist in Zoos today, was very

Figure 127

primitive indeed. It also seemed as if we Europeans were, perhaps, more interesting than the caged exhibits. (Fig 127)

We arrived in Singapore, in March 1956. At first we were housed in temporary accommodation at a location called "The Gap", off the South Buona Vista Road, near Pasir Panjang. This was a very hilly region of Singapore Island and the South Buona Vista Road was renowned for its sharp turns, many of them hairpins. The Singapore Motor Club, whose membership consisted mainly of British Forces personnel and expatriates, used to close the road for organised motor rallies, sprint races and speed trials. I recall one of their events when a driver was badly injured, if not killed. The road was also infamous for illegal drag racing

Figure 128

that was a hazard to normal traffic (Fig 128). Our temporary quarters were close to the start of the uphill section of South Buona Vista Road and that is probably why we were moved to Rochester Park soon after arriving there. Our proper married quarters were at No 3 Rochester Park. (Fig 129). It was a substantial house, of the type that are now known as 'the black and white bungalows'. It had a balcony that ran along the length of the first floor overlooking its sizeable gardens to the rear, with external stairs at each end. Beyond, across a road, we could see an Army barracks with a parade ground, the name of which escapes me. Quite often, in the cool of an evening, we would

Figure 129

often hear a military band playing as the musicians practised playing and marching manoeuvrers on the parade ground.

Figure 130

Today, there are not many of the *Black and White* bungalows left. Those that do remain are now highly sought after accommodation.(Fig 130)

Whilst on this tour of duty, Tom was engaged in examining the working efficiency of the Engineer Base Workshops (FARELF). The Workshops were defined by the War Office as being for :-

a)*The maintenance and repair, when required, of all Engineer stores and Equipment, including Plant which are beyond the capacity of the holding engineer unit.*

b)The production or repair of any Engineer Stores or Equipment. where provision or repair by usual means is not practicable by reason of time factor, etc.

c) Production of experimental prototypes.

d) Trade testing of Military and Civilian personnel within FARELF.

Figure 131

Tom's 52 page report (plus Appendices A to J and Annex I) is dated 10th July 1956. It makes quite uncomfortable reading regarding the lack of training, organisation and suitability of the management at the workshops. (Fig 131) Here the Far Eastern Army's equipment was constructed and repaired, including pontoons and bridging. His recommendation included sending some of the personnel

143

back to Long Marston, in England, for the appropriate specialist training courses. He also made a scathing assessment of the quality of materials supplied for use in the workshops, particularly that of *"Red Meranti which splits badly at points where nails and screws are used, and reacts chemically, corroding any iron or steel".*

The climate in Singapore was quite tropical, indeed very steamy at times. As children, we were collected daily for the school run by a three ton Army lorry from outside

Figure 132

the house, in Rochester Park. Pick up was at 0800 and we were returned around 1300 for our 'daily nap' in the heat of the day. Sometimes, the family went up to the Gillman Swimming Club in the afternoon or early evening to enjoy the pool and high diving boards. Tom was a very proficient swimmer, since gaining his London Schools Swimming Association 1st Class certificate in 1928. He also greatly enjoyed diving and the "swallow dive" from the high board was his party piece. We also partook in the delicious tea and toasted ham sandwiches that were by the served poolside. (Fig 132)

On one occasion we visited Haw Par Villa that was sited on the hill side of Pasir Panjang. It was also known as the Tiger

144

Balm Gardens, and named after the ointment created by Aw Boon Haw. Haw Par Villa depicts the *Ten Courts of Hell* from Chinese folklore and is home to more than 1,000 statues and 150 dioramas that depict surreal scenes of what happens if you should happen go there. (Fig 133)

As a child, I found it quite unnerving as many of scenes depicted forms of torture including disembowelling and the burning victims alive. The website now advises "Hell's Museum is not suitable for children under 9". I suspect it was a good place to show children what would happen if they didn't behave!

Figure 133

When we went in the 1950s, just outside the entrance gates there was an ice-cream seller where you could buy a Durian flavoured lolly. They were described by my Father as *"tasting like heaven but smelling like hell"* and he was right. When I visited Haw Par Villa again, in 2013, an ice-cream seller was still positioned there by the gates, but I didn't try a Durian lolly for a second time.

Following Singapore's return to British rule, after the Japanese occupation in WW2, the colony was in a very poor shape. Britain had inherited a legacy of rampant crime, poor health, corruption and widespread infrastructure damage. The fall of Singapore to the Japanese had seriously undermined the local view of British rule. There were increasing calls for self-rule on the Malayan peninsula by the Malayan Communist Party (MCP) which also spread to Singapore Island. Britain declared *The Malayan Emergency* in 1948, when the communist revolt began to take hold. This emergency lasted until 1960 and during this time over 1440 British personnel were killed during the insurrection. Both the Alvis Saracen (Fig 134) an armoured troop carrier and the Saracen (an armoured gun vehicle) were developed for responding to this emergency. Fighting in terrain that included rubber plantations, where the trees were planted in rows, these vehicles had to be no wider than 8ft and offer protection from ambush. Tom had an involvement in the construction of what he called "Q" vehicles.

Figure 134

These were three ton lorries disguised to look like ordinary troop carriers, but which concealed both protection and armaments under their canvas tops. They were used in the Army convoys when in action against the communists up on the Malay peninsula, probably complimenting the Saracen troop carriers. A number of disguised fighting platforms were created in WW2 that were also named with the prefix 'Q. They included merchant ships that were intended to lure U Boats to the surface, where they could be attacked. It seems quite likely that that nomenclature 'Q' could be a further reference point for Ian Fleming's so named fictional character in the James Bond series of books

Figure 135

On this tour, Tom was also involved with the construction of an access road during his tenure in Singapore and several photos of it were in his bag. Unfortunately, these construction photos do not give any detail as to where the road is actually routed. However, the local workers pictured in them may be seen carrying material by yokes (Fig 135).

There were several Bailey bridges along the road's route. These were probably a 'quick fix' before more permanent structures were built. (Fig 136)

Figure 136

By the mid 1950s a British commission decided that partial self government was the way forward for Singapore and gradually self rule was introduced, in stages. Not long before we returned to the UK, there was an increased threat to the British, and the service families, by the Communist insurgents.

Side arms were not usually carried by my father, but I do remember him coming home early one day to show my mother how to use a service revolver. Having shown her how to hold and fire it, he placed the revolver in the drawer of the hallway table of No 3 Rochester Park. His instruction to my mother was "*If anyone comes into the house - shoot first and we'll ask questions afterwards !*" We children were forbidden to touch the drawer by Tom - "o*r it will be six of the best with my stick*". His stick was the 'swagger stick' that he held under his left arm, when in uniform.

For his service in Malaya, Tom was awarded the General Service Medal with "Malaya" Clasp. For the servicemen and women, in Colony of Singapore, the qualifying period period for this was between 16 June 1948 and 31 January 1959.

Chapter 12

Western Command, No 1 E.S.D. Plant Troop

We returned to the UK in April 1957 and Tom was temporarily *"posted to RE Depot"*.

In July 1957 he was appointed Technical Staff Officer II (T.S.O. II) at the Inspectorate of Electrical and Mechanical Engineering (I.E.M.E.), followed by a similar post at the Inspectorate of Fighting Vehicles (I.F.V.) based at Kidbrooke, in Kent. Nothing is known of what he actually did there. However, as the wind-down and closure of I.F.V. was being planned he was being headhunted for another post, as evidenced by a string of correspondence in late 1960 between the Director of Standardisation (F.W.Hornsby) and the Deputy Master-General of the Ordnance (D.M.G.O.) asking for Tom to be re-allocated to the newly formed Standardisation Directorate. However it was denied, despite Tom's obvious interest and suitability for the role. (Fig 137)

It is understood that Major T.J. Goodman R.E., at present a TSO II on the staff of D.I.F.V.M.E. at Kidbrooke, may shortly be available for re-allocation of duties. If this is so he would be an admirable choice since his contact with standardization extends over some years (it includes membership of the ASRC and several Defence Specification Committees); this experience together with the fact that he is known to be an able and conscientious officer would be a most valuable asset to the Directorate.

Figure 137

The Inspectorate of Fighting Vehicles was transferred to the War Office in 1962, following the abolition of the Ministry of Supply in 1959 and then subsequently to the Ministry of Aviation. It was redesignated the Inspectorate of Fighting Vehicles and Mechanical Equipment (I.F.V.M.E.). With the formation of the Ministry of Defence Procurement Executive in 1971 the inspectorate was retitled Quality Assurance Directorate (Fighting Vehicles and Engineering Equipment) QAD (FE).

So, Tom had a brief posting to the Army Cataloguing unit in mid 1961, before his final posting in October 1961, to become the Commanding Officer of No 1 E.S.D. Plant Troop, back at Long Marston. The very place where he was posted to, upon his initial commission after volunteering for Bomb Disposal in 1941.

There were several interesting episodes during Tom's final posting back at Long Marston.

In 1963 there was a very severe winter that caused many parts of the United Kingdom to be snowed in. In Wales, strong Blizzards cut off many of the outlying villages and the Army was called in to assist in clearing the roads. Tom's unit was equipped with bulldozers, graders and other heavy earth moving plant and they were despatched to assist with giving access to the emergency services and local people around Brecon where there had been dumps of up to 10ft of snow. (Fig 138)

Figure 138

Also in the early 1960s, Tom and his Plant troop were involved with the project to restore the Stratford Canal Basin that was situated alongside the Royal Shakespeare Theatre, Stratford Upon Avon. This involved Tom's Troop in various exercises, including dredging the canal and basin, lifting new / repaired lock gates into place at various locks along the canal. The works involved some 'inmates' from Wormwood Scrubs and Birmingham prisons, one of whom was caught trying to sell one of Dad's (the Army's) pieces of heavy equipment. He was subsequently sent to court and received an extended stay at H.M.P.! The restoration project was completed in 1964. H.M. Queen Elizabeth, The Queen Mother officially opened the waterway on the 11th July 1964. (Fig 139)

My parents were invited to the formal opening. As a family, we went to Stratford Upon Avon. My Father and mother were guests on the Royal canal boat party and travelled a short length of the canal after the official opening ribbons

Figure 139

had been cut by H.M. In the evening my parents attended a special performance of Henry V at the Royal Shakespeare Theatre, in the presence of H.M. The family stayed at The Shakespeare Hotel, in Stratford, a timbered building that creaked and groaned as the floors were walked on. Apparently it was haunted, but we saw no Ghosts.

For attending The Queen Mother's canal boat opening party, Ivy (Mum) got a new hat. (Fig 140)

Figure 140

On the small foot bridge that crosses the Stratford canal, as it enters the basin (Fig 139), there is a small plaque recognising the work of those involved in work on the restoration project. (Fig 141)

Figure 141

The Army's Castlemartin Training Area (tank gunnery), in Pembrokeshire, was established in 1938 from both deserted and inhabited farmland and from parts of the defunct Cawdor Estate. The ranges were abandoned by the military soon after the Second World War, but were then re-instated in 1951 when the Korean War started.

In 1961 there was a shortage of suitable tank training areas in the northern part of Germany for the then recently reactivated German Tank Units. The British Army of the Rhine (BAOR) extensively used the ranges at the Bergen-Hohne Training Area which totalled 72,000 acres as their training demands could not be met by the limited acreage available in the United Kingdom. Therefore, a NATO accordance was agreed in Paris whereby the fledgling German forces could use the 5,000-acre range at Castlemartin. This relationship between the German Armoured Units and Castlemartin lasted until October 1996 when, after Germany reunification, additional ranges in eastern Germany became available.

Castlemartin, in Pembrokeshire, is one of only two armoured fighting vehicle ranges in the UK with direct live firing gunnery exercises and armoured vehicle manoeuvres. The other is Lulworth Cove. Castlemartin is the only Defence Training Area normally available for armoured units to fire live rounds on land and littoral environments including live firing into the sea. Tom was involved with the construction of a moving target railway for the Castlemartin range in 1963/4. This photo shows him giving instructions to one of his troop, during the construction phase of Block House No 6B on that railway.

(Fig 142)

Figure 142

Tom was also involved in the The Lower Swansea valley project, in the lower half of the valley of the River Tawe, South Wales. It runs from approximately the level of Clydach down to Swansea docks, where it opens into Swansea Bay and the Bristol Channel. This relatively small area was a focus of industrial innovation and invention during the Industrial Revolution, leading to a transformation of the landscape and a rapid rise in the population and economy of Swansea.

Today, the area is in the final stages of regeneration. Modern Industrial units and housing has replaced the pollution of the metallurgical industry and the area is now the home of Championship football club Swansea City A.F.C. and Welsh Rugby Union team The Ospreys.

Railway lines which criss-crossed the valley have now been replaced by walking and cycling paths and the River Tawe now hosts canoeists instead of copper carrying barges.

Over a period of about 150 years up until the 1920s, the open valley of the River Tawe became one of the most heavily industrialised and badly polluted areas in the developed world. (Fig 143)

Figure 143

There were a number of reasons that favoured the great expansion of industry in this particular location. The general exploitation of coal in the South Wales coalfield of the South Wales valleys had revealed seams of steam coal and anthracite close to the surface in the Upper Swansea valley and these were easily exploited by shallow drift mining or open cast mining. Smelting metals required more than three parts of coal to every one part of metal ore, so it was a major economic benefit to have high quality coal easily available. Swansea also had a good port and safe anchorage. The combination of these two factors meant that it was financially more viable to bring the ore to Swansea's coal than take the coal to the ore. In addition, the very high tidal ranges at Swansea allowed deep draught ships to access the river mouth. This allowed large quantities of raw materials to be brought in (allowing further profit through economies of scale) and, more importantly, the finished products, such as sheet copper, tinplate, alum, porcelain and coal to be exported.

The extent and scale of the industrialisation that took place at a time when there were almost no environmental controls in place which meant they created a legacy of chronic contamination of land and water by a great range of toxic and dangerous pollutants. The River Tawe was already being polluted by the coal mining industry and suffered badly. Even worse affected was the stream that meandered through the lower half of the valley, the Nant y Fendrod. Records about the history of this stream are sparse but it appears likely that for over 100 years most of the water was taken from this stream to be used in industry and its channel became the repository of much of the liquid waste from the various industries. In addition rainfall seeping through the growing waste tips added further burdens of by-products and waste materials. Even in the 1980s when all the industry had long since disappeared the Nant y Fendrod was still very seriously contaminated by copper, iron, nickel, ammonia and many other contaminants.

The Lower Swansea Valley Project began in the early 1960s with the aim of seeking to reclaim the land. Over the next twenty years the entire community of the area became involved in restoring the land. Nearly all the old buildings were cleared, while only a very few of historic interest have been preserved.

Tom's Plant Troop went, in convoy, to Swansea to undertake elements of the clearance. (Fig 144) He was involved in the demolition of a number of the tall chimneys and I know he found their razing to the ground a particularly interesting part of exercise, as it used his previous demolition and pyrotechnic experience. I don't think the chimneys always fell quite where he had predicted, but fortunately no one was injured in the process.

Figure 144

By April 1964, the initial stages of The Lower Swansea Valley Project were completed and Tom, together with the members of his R.E. Plant Troop, were invited to a civic reception by the Mayor of Swansea.

Note the error on the invitation that should have read "Royal Engineers, Plant Troop"(Fig 145)

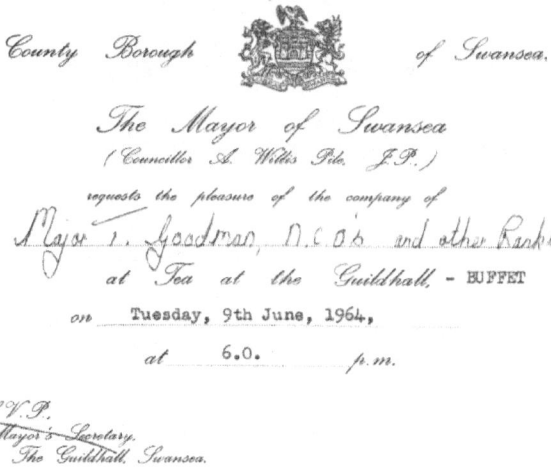

LOWER SWANSEA VALLEY PROJECT - ROYAL ENGINEERS PLANT TRAINING CAMP.

County Borough of Swansea.

The Mayor of Swansea
(Councillor A. Willis Pile, J.P.)

requests the pleasure of the company of

Major T. Goodman, N.C.O's and other Ranks

at Tea at the Guildhall - BUFFET

on Tuesday, 9th June, 1964,

at 6.0. p.m.

R.S.V.P.
Mayor's Secretary.
The Guildhall, Swansea.

Figure 145

A press photographer, from the South Wales Evening Post, was covering the Civic reception and took a photo of Tom with the Mayor, Mayoress and Town Clerk. Members of his troop are in the background. (Fig 146) Note - Tom is wearing spurs.

It was a very proud day for him and probably the last big project he was involved in.

Figure 146

Tom's retirement date was *London Gazetted for 29th September 1965*, after almost 37 years service with The Colours, when he was aged 50 and 9 months.

His Plant Troop presented him with a fine silver tankard, suitably engraved, that I keep safely today and occasionally fill with ale. He was also given a farewell 'mess dinner' by his brother officers at Long Marston, shortly before his retirement. Tom is on the left in (Fig 147).

In 1999 it was announced that the MOD were closing the Royal Engineer's Supply Depot at long Marston. It was subsequently redeveloped, including for housing and the storage of railway rolling stock on the extensive network of sidings.

Figure 147

Upon his retirement, Tom's Medal awards were- M.B.E. (Military), 1939 / 45 Star, The Defence Medal, The War Medal, The General Service Medal, with Malaya Clasp and The Coronation Medal 1953. He was also granted the honorary title of Major, R.E.

Tom was posthumously awarded the General Service Medal Canal Zone Clasp in 2019.

In the 1964 version of The Army List (page 640) Tom's seniority is No 4 amongst the Majors, on Extended Service, in the Corps of Royal Engineers.

Chapter 13 - The Retirement Years

Tom had been planning ahead for his retirement and had wanted to take a Retired Officer's post with the Ministry of Defence, which had been advertised in the February 1965 edition of the Royal Engineers Journal. It was a role dealing with the stores and equipment provisioned by the Royal Engineers, at a salary of £1,285. He would appear to have been very well qualified to undertake that role and, on the side lines, Tom had been encouraged to apply for it. In the event, he was "ruled out" for that job because he was still eligible for recall on the Army's "active list". However, the Army did offer to Extend his Service for another 3 year term, but he declined to accept it. (Fig 148)

Sir,

With reference to your letter dated 1st March 1965, I am directed to inform you that it is noted with regret that you do not wish to accept the extension of Service offered you under this office letter P/173594/AG7(O) dated 19th January 1965.

Accordingly, your Service under the Extended Service Scheme will now terminate on 28th September 1965, and action will be taken in due course by the Military Secretary to effect the relinquishment of your commission on 29th September 1965.

Figure 148

I clearly remember Tom talking to my mother about being "ruled out", expressing that he was quite unhappy with the whole scenario and that the time had come to make provision for his future outside of the Army, because "*the older I get the more difficult it will be to get a job in civvy street"*.

As it so happens, in the same edition of that Royal Engineers Journal, another post was advertised (by Lt. Col. Edwards) for an Export Packing Technical Manager at L.E.P. Packing Ltd, based in Chiswick, West London. This post was concerned with *"the packing and preservation of all types of machinery and electronic equipment for transport and storage by all media under all conditions throughout the World". Starting salary £1,250."*

Tom applied for the post and was duly appointed. He started at L.E.P. immediately after "leaving The Colours" in September 1965.

For the first year Tom commuted daily to Chiswick, by car, from our flat in Crofton Park. In September 1966 we said farewell to Crofton Park and moved to a comfortable house at 120 Sutton Court Road, Chiswick, W4 3EQ, located on the corner of Sutton Court Road and Staveley Road. It was purchased from Tom's Army Retirement gratuity. (Fig 149)

Staveley Road was well known for its avenue of mature Cherry Blossom Trees that gave a beautiful display each spring. Queen Elizabeth The Queen Mother, when en-route nearby, was often driven discreetly down it in

Figure 149

order to see the Cherry Blossom trees when they flowered in the spring. It is also rumoured that the Cherry Blossom shoe polish derived its name from those trees in Staveley Road.

For Tom it was just a 15 minute walk to work at L.E.P., from "120". In summer, he often came home at lunch time for a sandwich and to sit and enjoy the garden with Ivy, my mother.

At some point in the late 1960s, Tom came home one Friday evening and suggested I went with him to his works the following morning. He said there was something there that I might be interested to see, without wanting to elaborate any further. So, on the Saturday morning I accompanied him. There, in the L.E.P. works yard, was John Lennon's famous Rolls Royce (Fig 150). Tom handed me the keys and said I could take it for a spin round the yard. It was a real surprise and great fun to drive. Until then, the only car I had driven was Tom's Morris Oxford - with L Plates on ! The Rolls was being crated up the following Monday morning, for immediate shipping to New York, USA. Tom had designed a special packing crate to suit it.

Figure 150

In 1970, Tom's post at L.E.P. was declared Redundant. Quite what had transpired I am not sure, but there was a suggestion, at home, that one of the other more senior managers had asked Tom to sign off some of his expenses. Tom had gratefully declined to do so, as he hadn't a clue whether they were legitimate, or not, and it wasn't long after that Tom's left L.E.P. However, Tom soon found another post at The National Physical Laboratory, Teddington. He joined the Property Services Agency, Building Services staff, looking after the various engineering services that supported the site's operation. The National Physical Laboratory was established in 1900 at Bushy House in Teddington, on the site of the Kew Observatory. Its purpose was "*for standardising and verifying instruments, for testing materials, and for the determination of physical constants*". The laboratory was run by the UK government, with members of staff being part of the civil service. It grew to fill a large selection of buildings on the Teddington site. Tom is seated at the desk, right, Tom is seated at the desk, right (Fig 151)

Figure 151

In early 1972, Tom suffered a serious heart attack at work in his office, at Teddington, which kept him off work for several months. In April 1973, Tom transferred to the Property Services Agency at the Department of the Environment, based at Chadwick Street, SW1. His post there was Planned Maintenance Officer and he quickly established himself as "*an upright and honourable man*". He was then working within a few hundred yards of the embankment and the wartime H.Q. of the Secret Service M.O.I.(SP) that he was a member of back in WW2.

Also in "Civvy Street", Tom was a UK representative on a European Standards Committee. (Fig 152).

Quite what the committee was dealing with, I am not sure, but he seemed suitably interested. Note his hand on chin stance.

Figure 152

At about 0730 on the morning of Monday 21st October 1974, Tom came to check I was soon leaving for work. He then left home himself to catch the District Line tube to Westminster. At about 0900 there was a knock at the front door of "120". There stood a policeman. He brought the news that Tom had collapsed on the District Line tube between Hammersmith and Earls Court stations. He had suffered a heart attack and died on the spot. That day the trains were delayed and although a few people were late for work, at least they got there and came home again.

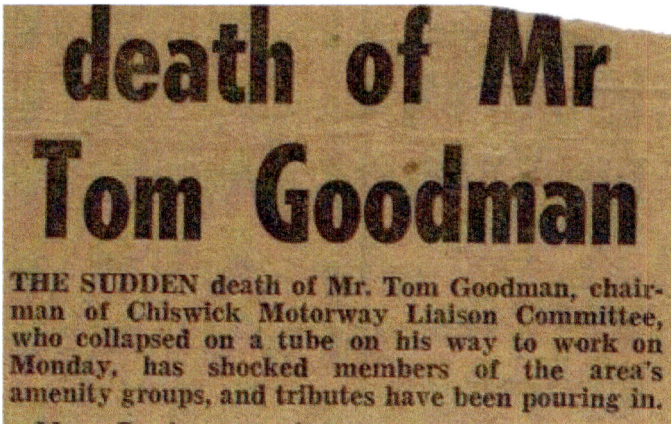

death of Mr Tom Goodman

THE SUDDEN death of Mr. Tom Goodman, chairman of Chiswick Motorway Liaison Committee, who collapsed on a tube on his way to work on Monday, has shocked members of the area's amenity groups, and tributes have been pouring in.

Figure 153

We received many letters of condolence on Tom's passing, including one from Barney Hayhoe M.P. There was also a front page obituary entitled "*Sudden Death of Mr Tom Goodman*" in the following Thursday's edition of The Chiswick Times. (Fig 153)

Tom had served on several local committees that were trying to protect Chiswick, including the historic Chiswick House, from being irreparably damaged by the Highway authority's plans to upgrade the A316, Chertsey Road, as a feeder road for the M3 motorway, from the Hogarth roundabout on the A4. He was Chairman of Chiswick Motorways Liaison Committee and Vice-Chairman of Chiswick House Residents Association (CHARA) and applied his engineering knowledge to help defeat the road upgrade proposals, including the use of tunnelling as a means to save hundreds of houses from being demolished. In the face of the strength of local opposition, the Highway authority's plans were dropped. Not long after this, Tom's parallel

Figure 154

campaign for a set of Traffic Lights at the Staveley Road and A316 junction, to slow down the London bound traffic was approved. They became known by his fellow conservationists as "Tom's lights".

A wooden park bench, bearing an engraved plaque marking Tom's contribution to local conservation, was purchased by CHARA and by subscriptions from other local supporters. It was sited in Chiswick House grounds by the Camellia House, where Tom often used to sit and picnic with my mother, in the sunshine. (Fig154)

I was on a Digital Techniques course at the BBC's Engineering Training Centre in Evesham, in the 1970s, not long after Tom had died. One evening I took the Training Centre's shuttle bus down to the BBC Club, that was

Figure 155

located in Evesham town itself (Fig 155). After a game, or two, of skittles I went for a stroll to explore the town and

Figure 156

stopped at a pub I had seen before called The Olde Swanne Inne. (Fig 156) Once inside, I spied a shield on the wall behind the bar with The Royal Engineers emblem on it. I asked the elderly landlady how it came to be there. She explained that a group of Officers from the Long Marston Army Depot often used to hold their social meetings in *The Olde Swanne Inne* and they had presented the shield to her as a token of thanks for her hospitality. The Landlady even remembered Tom's name and she commented on my close resemblance to him. I have often been told of my having a close resemblance to Tom. Given his personal achievements, it has been my humble honour to bear that load.

Chapter 14 - UXB Film Synopsis

A synopsis of the 1941 Army Kinematograph Service film 'UXB' follows :-

It opens with a long shot of a town burning, actors protect themselves as bombs fall, aeroplanes overhead, whining of bombs. Dramatisation of an old woman found in bombed out house by ARP warden. She will not leave. The next morning the ARP warden returns to inspect damage and a bomb explodes. Appearances can be deceptive; how to check for traces of a blast ie. four garages are destroyed but nearby windows are intact as is the drainpipe thereby implying a UXB may be present. Armed forces, civil defence and police must know about this for accurate reconnaissance is necessary (*Tom appears in this sequence at approximately 3 min and 30sec into the film*). The range of German HE bombs is examined in detail; the thin-cased SC bomb with cross- section diagram for destruction over a wide area of property; armour piercing or SD bomb which explodes on impact and targets battleships, power stations, factories and steel reinforced buildings also with cross-section diagram. A detailed description of each SC bomb by colour, size and weight. How to identify a German bomb by parts found at sites eg. tail fins, tail drum, cone, kopf ring, carrying bands, lug. A detailed description of SD bombs by colour, size and weight. Bomb reconnaissance outlines size of crater, type of crater and surrounding damage made by particular types of bombs; diagram of bomb going underground and the dangers this presents ie. a build-up of carbon dioxide and possible explosion. Will the bomb explode? A section through the 50 kg bomb illustrates three stages of the fuze - gain, pick-up and charge. All German fuzes are electrical; diagrams and close-up of charge to explain workings of this. Four types of fuze - impact: instant; delay action: 250 kg and 500 kg bombs that can explode up to eighty hours after landing; booby trap: use of striker to detonate (with diagram); anti-handling: any vibration will set off reaction once it has landed. What must be done if a UXB is found? All buildings must be cleared within thirty yards; all rooms facing the bomb must be cleared within one hundred yards; outer doors and windows must be opened and the area should be roped off. Diagrams and maps explain this in more detail. Prioritising areas - A, B, C, D eg. A = industrialised area of munitions, factories, goods, gas works and power stations. Models of areas with UXB and procedure to prevent damage; UX parachute mines; anti-personnel bombs; diagrammatic breakdown of incendiary bomb container (holds thirty-six bombs); Molotov pantry (ten foot long holds seven hundred incendiaries), flash book, German flare casing (parachute plus one to four candles), UX ack-ack shells, aeroplane cannon shells and bomb with board and ring and piano wire. Procedure of reporting an UXB. Documentary of munitions factories, underground station on the Northern line, commuters; German film of bombers taking off for England; flashes on screen, London burning and clearing up the mess. Civil defence's role in conjunction with the army in dealing with UXB - the chain of reporting in diagrammatic form; who to report to, forms etc; dramatisation of events from the bomb landing , evacuation of the area, reporting the UXB, bomb reconnaissance and eventual defusing. Dramatisation of priority "A" UXB threatening P.O. cables and the measures taken to evacuate the area to make the bomb safe; a UXB in the back garden - the ARP warden thinks it is a large bomb, closer inspection reveals it is not - the need to reconnoitre carefully is constantly emphasised to avoid wasting resources and time; a priority "A" UXB is found at a shunting yard where the usual procedure is followed although the bomb disposal officer realises that normal activities may be partly resumed while the bomb is deactivated. Final reiteration of reconnaissance, reporting, prioritising and categorising before action.

Chapter 15 - Acknowledgements

My vote of thanks for their kind assistance in this endeavour goes to following organisations:

The Army Historical Branch, City of Dunkirk, Foynes Flying Boat Museum, Imperial War Museum, M.O.D. Records Section, National Archives Australia, National WW2 Museum USA, Poole Flying Boats, Scout Association of Malta, San Diego Air & Space Museum, Selsey Public Library, Singapore Motor Club, S.O.E. Interest Group, Wikipedia.

and the following individuals :

Mike Allisstone, Tim Alexander, Malcom Atkin, David Armstrong, Julian Barnard, Tom Colville, Reg Danford-Cordingly, Will Davies, John Friberg, Sue Goodenough, Barbara Goodman, Sheryl Green, Joe Haynes, Stuart Ivinson, Fred Judge, Claire Jordan, Peter Markham, Gerry McArdle, Paul Sansom, Sue Stacey, Des Turner, Lt Col. Eric Wakeling, Eileen Willard and John Wright.

Lastly, and by no means least, thank you to my wife Margaret who has spent many hours, days and weeks wondering if I would ever manage to finish writing this account.

Chapter 16 - Reference List

Direct references to Tom are indicated in RED

Title	ISBN
The Army List 1964	
1940 War Office german-shells-fuzes-and-bombs	
1940 WO Bomb Disposal Manual (cover)	
1941 Bomb Rec. & Protection Against UXBs, Military Trg Pamphlet No 45	9781905973828
1941 Manual of Bomb Disposal (Index)1941	
1941 RAAF-Notes-on-Japanese-Bombs-and-Fuzes	
1941 sd2-butterfly	
1944 Australian Bomb Disposal Technical Instructions	
1952 Bomb Reconnaissance & Protection Against Unexploded Bombs	WO Code 8730
1953 tm-2-german-bombs-mines-igniters-and-grenades-1953	
Bomb Disposal in WW2	9781526715564
British Munitions, Recognition and Disposal (for Bomb Safety Officers)	9781783313617
Courage Beyond Duty	9781492932987
Danger UXB -The Complete Collection - 4 x DVD — Thames TV	5027626243944
Danger UXB – The Heroic Story of WW2 Bomb Disposal Teams	9781408701959
Danger UXB – The Remarkable Story of UXBs in WW2	9780752219383
Danger UXB 1979 (incs Manual of Bomb Disposal 1941)	0333257111
Disarming Hitler's V Weapons Bomb Disposal The V1 &V2 Rockets	1526781905
My London Bomb Squad	9780955282515
Operation Crossbow	1419844911
Photographic Story of War time Bomb Disposal	0952579901
The Danger of UXBs	9780952579922
The LCC Bomb Damage Maps	9780500518250
The Lonely War : Story of BD in WW2 by one who was there at the time	9780952579946
Time Stood Still in a Muddy Hole	9781785452864
Unexploded Bomb A History of Bomb Disposal	X000733512
UXB Malta -The Most Bombed Place on Earth	9780752466194
UXB- Unexploded Bombs on the Home Front 1941 -1944	5013929667259
V2, A Combat History of the First Ballistic Missile	1594160120
War Booklet Bomb Disposal Army Bureau - No 68 Self Preservation April 1944	
A Man Called Intrepid	0-7221-8166-3
The Irregulars, Roald Dahl and the British Spy Ring in Wartime Washington	97816075181811
Secret History of British Intelligence in the Americas 1940 -1945	9780880642361
Inside - Camp X, Top Secret WW2 Secret Agent Training School in Canada	0968706207
Camp X SOE and the American Connection	9780670817375
Assignment to Catastrophe, Vol 1, Prelude to Dunkirk July 1939 -May 1940	X001030020
The Flames of Calais	034010533x
Sword of Bone, The Phoney War and Dunkirk 1940	0727800418
Dunkirk, The British Evacuation 1940	0213165988
Dunkirk, The Storms of War	0715378570
The Miracle of Dunkirk	0713912111
Escape from Catastrophe, 1940 Dunkirk	0953435822
Dunkirk – Fight to The Last Man	9780141024370
Dunkirk – Retreat to Victory	9781509860043
Dunkirk 1940, Operation Dynamo	9781846034572
Dunkirk – Forgotten Voices	9780091932213
Oxford Companion to Australian Military History	0195532279
Australia in the War 1939-1945 Series 2 Vol	X000160784
Fall of Hong Kong	X002261820
Task Force 57, The BPF 1944-45	0947554858
The Fall of Hong Kong	0300103735

Battle for Hong Kong 1941-1945, Hostage to Fortune	1-86227-315-4
The British Pacific Fleet – The Royal Navy's Most Powerful Strike Force	9781526702838
The British Pacific & East Indies Fleets – The Forgotten Fleets -50th Anniv.	1-874447-28-4
British Military Intelligence, Objects from The Military Intelligence Museum	9781445662381
Operation Crossbow	9781848093072
Ocean Bridge: The History of Ferry Command	9781857800296
1942 Royal Engineers Demolitions Handbook	
Aston House Station 12 SOE Secret Centre (1st Edition)	0750942770
Battle of Britain Airfields of Group 11	1844151646
Behind Enemy Lines with SOE	9781526779748
Brighton's Secret Agents	9781910500750
Churchill and Tito, SOE, Bletchley Park and supporting Yugoslav in WW2	152670496X
Churchill's Ministry of Ungentlemanly Warfare	9781444798982
Churchill's White Rabbit, Story of a real life James Bond	9780752467481
Clandestine Warfare, Weapons and Equipment of the SOE and OSS	0713718226
Descriptive Cat. of Special Devices & Supplies, SOE	9781977621405
Forgotten Voices of The Secret War – Inside History of SOE During WW2	978009191850
French resistance in Sussex	1-899174-02-8
Gubbins and SOE	0850520029
Heroines of SOE, F Section Britain's Secret Women in France	9780752456634
Jungle Fighter, Infantry Officer, Chindit & SOE Agent Burma 1941-45	1871085349
Memories of an SOE Historian	9780753195703
Now it Can be Told — 1 x DVD	9019322349983
Our Man in Malaya, SOE Force 136	9780750947107
Pioneers of Irregular Warfare – Secrets of Mil.Int.Research Dept. WW2	9781526766007
Sabotage & Subversion, Stories from The Files of SOE and OSS	185409260X
Sabotage and Subversion, The SOE and OSS at War	9780752457383
SAS & Special Forces, WW2 Secret Ops Handbook.	9781838860776
Secret Agent Selection : WW2 in 2 DVDs	DAZ00382
Secret Agent, Britain's Wartime Secret Service (Paper Back)	0563488115
Secret History of SOE THE Special Operations Executive 1940-45	1903608112
Secret War — DVD 1	5060294373643
Secret War — DVD 2	5060294373674
Secret War — DVD 3	5060294373650
Secret War — DVD 4	5060294373667
Secret War The Story of SOE Britain's Wartime Sabotage Organisation	0340518707
Secret War, A Pictorial Record of the SOE	1840672919
Secret Warriors – Hidden Heroes of MI6, OSS M19, SOE & SAS	9780853643937
Section D for Destruction	9781473892606
Setting France Ablaze, SOE in France During WW2	1783463368
Shadow Warriors, Daring Missions of WW2 by Women of OSS & SOE	9781445661445
SOE An Outline History of SOE 1940-1946	0712665854
SOE and The Resistance	9781441119711
SOE Churchill's Secret Agents	9781784420406
SOE in the Far East	0192851683
SOE Recollections and Reflections 1940-45	0370304044
SOE Secret Weapons Centre Station 12 (2nd Edition)	9780752459448
SOE Special Operations Executive 1940-1946	563201932
SOE Syllabus, Lessons in Ungentlemanly Warfare World War II	1-903365-60-0
SOE The Scientific Secrets	075094005
SOE's Mastermind An Authorised Biography of Maj Gen Gubbins	9781526796493
SOE's Ultimate Deception, Operation PERIWIG	9780750940276
Special Operations Executive Manual, How to be an Agent in Occupied Europe	9780008103613
Tangmere and The SOE	
The Art of Guerilla Warfare, May 1939	9781976334627
The British Spy Manual – The Authentic S.O.E. Guide for WWII	9781781314029
The Secret Ministry of AG, & Fish, My life in Churchill's School for Spies	9780230770904
The Secret War of Charles Fraser-Smith : The Gadget Wizard of WW2	9780952840800
The Secrets of Station 14 Briggens House	9780750996198
They Also Serve, An SOE Agent in the WRNS	0709077157

They Fought Alone : The Story of British agents in France   9781849546928
Twins, The SOEs Brothers of Vengeance   9780750989831
Undercover Operator, Wartime Experiences with SOE in France and Far East   753193418
Undercover:Men and Women of the Special Operations Executive   9780099668206
Unearthing Churchill's Secret Army   9781399013208
With SOE in Greece, The Wartime experiences of Captain Pat Evans   1526725134
Within Two Cloaks Missions with SIS and SOE   0718300270
Aston House Station XII – E.S.6. (WD), Aston Village History Series No1
Secret Agent, Britain's Wartime Secret Service (Hard Back)   563537345
Between Silk and Cyanide   9780750948357
1946 SRD Technical Handbook Vol 4
Special Operations Australia Vol 1 – Organisation   9781461140924
Special Operations Australia Vol 2 – Operations   9781461196518
Special Operations Australia Vol 3 – Communications   9781463673512
The SRD Technical Handbook, Weapons & Equipment of Z Special Unit 9781478175742
They Came Unseen : The Men & Women of Special Unit Z (Australia)   9781876179175
Z Special Unit: The Elite Allied World War 2 Guerilla Force   9781472847096

Printed in Great Britain
by Amazon